HBR Guide to
Dealing with Conflict

Harvard Business Review Guides

Arm yourself with the advice you need to succeed on the job, from the most trusted brand in business. Packed with how-to essentials from leading experts, the HBR Guides provide smart answers to your most pressing work challenges.

The titles include:

HBR Guide to Being More Productive

HBR Guide to Better Business Writing

HBR Guide to Building Your Business Case

HBR Guide to Buying a Small Business

HBR Guide to Coaching Employees

HBR Guide to Data Analytics Basics for Managers

HBR Guide to Delivering Effective Feedback

HBR Guide to Emotional Intelligence

HBR Guide to Finance Basics for Managers

HBR Guide to Getting the Right Work Done

HBR Guide to Leading Teams

HBR Guide to Making Every Meeting Matter

HBR Guide to Managing Stress at Work

HBR Guide to Managing Up and Across

HBR Guide to Negotiating

HBR Guide to Office Politics

HBR Guide to Performance Management

HBR Guide to Persuasive Presentations

HBR Guide to Project Management

HBR Guide to
Dealing with Conflict

Amy Gallo

HARVARD BUSINESS REVIEW PRESS

Boston, Massachusetts

Copyright 2017 Harvard Business School Publishing Corporation

The web addresses referenced in this book were live and correct at the
time of the book's publication but may be subject to change.

Library of Congress Cataloging-in-Publication Data

Names: Gallo, Amy, author.
Title: HBR guide to dealing with conflict / by Amy Gallo.
Other titles: Harvard Business Review guide to dealing with conflict |
    Harvard business review guides.
Description: Boston, Massachusetts : Harvard Business Review Press,
    [2017] | Series: Harvard Business Review guides
Identifiers: LCCN 2016044710 | ISBN 9781633692152 (pbk. :
    alk. paper)
Subjects: LCSH: Conflict management. | Work environment.
Classification: LCC HD42 .G33 2017 | DDC 658.4/053--dc23 LC
    record available at https://lccn.loc.gov/2016044710

ISBN: 9781633692152
eISBN: 9781633692169

The paper used in this publication meets the requirements of the
American National Standard for Permanence of Paper for Publications
and Documents in Libraries and Archives Z39.48-1992.

What You'll Learn

While some of us enjoy a lively debate with colleagues and others prefer to suppress our feelings over disagreements, we all struggle with conflict at work. Every day we navigate an office full of competing interests, clashing personalities, limited time and resources, and fragile egos. Sure, we share the same goals as our colleagues, but we don't always agree on how to achieve them. We work differently. We rub each other the wrong way. We jockey for position. But disagreements don't have to be a source of unhealthy tension. So how can you deal with conflict in a way that is both professional and productive—where it improves both your work and your relationships? This guide lays out a straightforward process for addressing nebulous situations. You start by understanding whether you generally seek or avoid conflict, identifying the most frequent reasons for disagreement, and knowing what approaches work for what scenarios. Then, if you decide to address your situation, you use that information to plan and conduct a productive conversation. Knowing there is a process to follow can make conflict more manageable. This guide will give you the advice you need to:

- Understand the most common sources of conflict

- Explore your options for addressing a disagreement

- Recognize whether you—and your counterpart— typically seek or avoid conflict

- Assess the situation that's making you feel uncomfortable

- Prepare for and engage in a difficult conversation

- Manage your and your counterpart's emotions

- Develop a resolution together

- Know when to walk away

- Repair relationships

Contents

Preface   ix

*Conflict at work is inevitable—but it doesn't
have to be destructive.*

BY LINDA HILL

Introduction: A Practical Plan for Dealing with Conflict   xvii

Take it step by step.

SECTION ONE

Preparing for Conflict Before It Happens

1. **Types of Conflict**   3

   Identify the source.

2. **Your Options for Handling Conflict**   15

   *Different situations call for different
   approaches.*

3. **Recognize Your Natural Tendency**   31

   Most of us fall into one of two camps.

Contents

SECTION TWO

Managing a Conflict

4. **Assess the Situation**   43

   *Understand the players and the larger
   context.*

5. **Get Ready for the Conversation**   61

   Don't rush in.

6. **Have a Productive Conversation**   75

   Listen and be heard.

SECTION THREE

Resolving a Conflict

7. **Get to a Resolution and Make a Plan**   101

   Collaborate to find a creative solution.

8. **Repair the Relationship**   111

   Rebuild trust and move on.

9. **Navigate Common Situations**   121

   What to do if . . .

Sources   165
Featured Experts   175
Index   185
About the Author   193

Preface

by Linda Hill

Years ago, a colleague and I got into a fight. I had been selected to lead a cross-functional task force to review a portion of our MBA curricula. This was a diverse group of people—a few fellow junior faculty, people from other departments, and professors who had been at the school for decades, including my senior colleague and friend, whom I'll call Elizabeth. I was a brand-new tenured professor, and although I was surprised that I'd been picked to lead the team, I was also honored. And I was glad that I would be able to rely on Elizabeth for her expertise. After all, she had much more experience than I did.

Yet each time the group met, Elizabeth wasn't participating. She sat silently and rarely, if ever, had anything positive to contribute. We'd be talking about a topic that I knew she had an opinion on, and still she didn't say anything.

When she did open her mouth, it was to disparage me. In front of the group, she picked on what I felt were trivial things, like the fact that I didn't have all the supplemental materials in the same order as they were listed in the agenda. I could tell that something was wrong.

So could the rest of the team. People exchanged glances when Elizabeth openly criticized me for not being prepared. Some people tried to jump in and move things along when things got tense between us. But it was clear that the situation was making the whole team uncomfortable—me, Elizabeth, and everybody else.

I was confounded. Elizabeth and I had always gotten along, and whenever we'd collaborated in the past, it went well. After a few weeks of enduring her alternating silent treatment and carping, I decided to talk to her. I closed her office door behind me, sat down, and asked, "We aren't really working well together, are we?"

I wasn't prepared for what came next. She started yelling at me. She thought that I was doing a horrible job of running the group, that we weren't making progress on the evaluation, and that I was wasting her and everyone else's time. I felt backed into a corner, and as a result, I raised my voice, too, defending myself against her accusations.

This was not a smart way to handle the situation. It quickly became clear that neither of us wanted to be fighting. I didn't know what to do. I was concerned that without Elizabeth on board, the group would never be able to finish our work. And more importantly, I worried that Elizabeth's and my relationship, a relationship that I valued, was going to be irreparably damaged. And she didn't seem to be doing any better.

I'm not proud of what I did—you should never raise your voice at people at work. It felt horrible at the time; I was exasperated, angry, upset, questioning myself and Elizabeth. But our disagreement over who should be in charge of the group, how it should be run, and whose expertise needed to be tapped and in what way was not necessarily negative in and of itself. These questions needed to be addressed for the group to do its best work and for me to be effective as a leader.

During our heated exchange we got those issues out into the open. But how we handled that initial discussion was problematic—we weren't going to solve the issues we'd raised if we were both defensive. We needed to work together.

And that's just the thing—conflict at work is going to happen, no matter what you do. And it should. It can be good for you, your team, and your organization. But how you deal with it can make the difference between a negative interaction and a productive one.

That's why you've turned to this guide. We don't want to have screaming matches with colleagues. We don't want to feel as if our projects will fail unless we give in to what someone else wants. We don't want to lose sleep over an intense interaction. We *want* to better understand why conflict happens, our options for addressing it, and how to navigate these disagreements so that we end up with our dignity and relationships intact.

Imagine how things with Elizabeth would've gone if I hadn't just waltzed into her office and confronted her. What if I had thought through the discussion in advance, considering what Elizabeth and I were actually disagreeing about, and thinking about our different personalities? What if I had chosen the right time and place for us to talk, framed my message carefully, heard her out, and explained my position? Or what if Elizabeth had come to me earlier and explained why she wasn't participating, made clear that her issues weren't personal but had to do with how I was running the group or what the team was trying to achieve? Instead of sitting there staring at each other, fuming, we might've been engaged in a thoughtful, productive discussion.

Learning to navigate conflicts such as the one I had with Elizabeth is not really a choice in today's organizations. There's always going to be diversity, interdependence, and competition over scarce resources. And that's not a bad thing. When passionate people with different perspectives collaborate to address a problem or an opportunity, there can be give-and-take and productive disagreement. That healthy competition helps create better products, features, and solutions. The research on innovation is clear: Without "creative abrasion" you won't have a robust marketplace of new ideas. The most effective people are those who can disagree constructively, not destructively, and keep difficult conversations substantive, not personal.

Thankfully, mercifully really, in the middle of our fight, Elizabeth paused and asked if I wanted to get coffee with her across campus. Not sure what else to do, I agreed.

The change of scenery was exactly what we needed. As we walked across campus, we both calmed down and Elizabeth opened up about the source of her frustrations. It turns out that I was driving her crazy. I'm not a linear thinker and she is. The process I was using was infuriating to her. She wanted to know how each step led to the next, and I was willing to let things evolve more organically. Plus she felt as if I wasn't using her expertise. I assumed people would speak up if they had ideas—that those with the most experience, such as Elizabeth, would chime in when they wanted to, so I didn't call on anyone in particular and never met with individual team members outside the group to get their perspective. By not calling on her, or openly acknowledging her expertise and asking for her opinion, I had upset her. She felt that I hadn't shown her enough respect. It's not that I didn't feel it (in fact, I assumed that she assumed that I respected her), but I didn't demonstrate it.

Perhaps what really got me in trouble was that I hadn't tried to see the situation from her perspective. I didn't think about how she might feel having someone with far less experience be in charge of something she cared about so much.

We didn't see eye to eye on how the committee should be managed—and she felt mistreated. We both were unafraid of conflict and typically approached it head-on, which is why we ended up in such a heated exchange in her office.

Her complaints made me realize that perhaps others in the group were having similar reactions. I wasn't

adapting my style for what worked best for the team—
I was doing what was most comfortable to me. Also, I
had assumed that by virtue of holding the leadership position, I had credibility. I didn't think I needed to earn
everyone's trust, but I absolutely did.

Once we understood what exactly we were fighting
about, and we had heard each other out, we were able
to move toward a resolution. I asked for Elizabeth's advice. How would she run the group? I was a new leader,
and I wanted to learn from her. We both wanted the
same thing—to produce the best curricula for our students—and to get there, I vowed to be more respectful
of the wisdom and experience she brought to the group
and to be more explicit about the process I was using to
run the meetings. I started to ask her opinion before the
team met. If I thought there was something she wouldn't
agree with, I gave her a heads-up. And I started regularly
asking everyone to suggest options before we started
evaluating them so that we could objectively look at the
pros and cons.

Elizabeth made changes after our discussion, too.
She stopped nitpicking. She backed off and gave me
more space. Because everyone deeply respected her, the
change in her attitude influenced the group positively.
People were more at ease and offered ideas freely. Suggestions were no longer "Elizabeth's idea" or "Linda's
idea"; they were all viable options we could evaluate
based on their merits.

I was fortunate. I was able to preserve my relationship
with Elizabeth, and the task force's work was better as a
consequence of our fight.

Looking back, I wish I had had the advice in this book before I spoke to Elizabeth. I could've saved us both a lot of grief if I had better understood the common sources of conflict, how people approach it differently, and the various options and strategies for solving it.

That's what you'll get in the pages ahead. You'll learn how to effectively navigate conflicts with your boss, your peers, your direct reports, and partners outside your company. You'll do the foundational work of better understanding the different types of conflict, your own tendency toward approaching it, and your options for resolving it. Then you'll learn the process to follow when a specific conflict arises—from assessing what kind of conflict it is, to preparing for the conversation, to hearing your counterpart out, and to ultimately reaching a satisfying resolution and repairing your relationship, if necessary.

Mastering all of this will not absolve you from having fights at work. I still have them, for sure. We all do, and maybe on occasion you will lose your temper, say something ugly, and behave in a way that you regret. But by following the advice in this book, those occasions will be fewer and less painful—for you and your colleagues.

Introduction: A Practical Plan for Dealing with Conflict

Let's face it: There's no such thing as a conflict-free office. We fight at work. We disagree about how to implement a new IT system. We battle over which strategy to pursue. We engage in turf wars about who gets to lead the website redesign project. And sometimes, we just act like passive-aggressive jerks toward one another.

And as uncomfortable and draining as conflict can be, conflict in and of itself isn't really the problem. It's how we handle it that matters.

Consider these two fictional stories:

Celia and her colleague, Sara, disagreed about how to word an important provision in a client contract. As the legal expert, Celia felt Sara's suggestion was too vague and perhaps even intentionally deceptive to the customer—implying better payment terms than their company was willing to allow. When Celia pointed out how the language might be misinterpreted, Sara stood her ground. Celia knew that this was an important customer for the company, and the CEO was eagerly awaiting news that the deal was closed, so she let it go. But she worried for several weeks whether she should've pushed harder. She lost sleep over it, avoided Sara at the office, and dreaded the date when the customer would receive its first invoice. And rightly so—when that time came, the customer was extremely unhappy and Celia ended up with Sara in the CEO's office having an all-out fight over whose fault it was. The two colleagues didn't speak for weeks afterward, and it took months for Celia's manager to regain trust that she could handle important contracts.

Now, let's take a look at what happened with a manager named Antonio.

Antonio had always had a positive relationship with his boss, Rebecca, but lately he noticed that she was frequently talking over him. As soon as Antonio started to say something, Rebecca would interrupt, often dismissing his view and presenting an opposing one. Antonio was annoyed. He wanted to pull Rebecca aside and tell her to quit it. But before doing that, he spent some time trying to understand what was going on and seeing things from Rebecca's perspective. He knew that she wasn't afraid of conflict and that she might not see her behavior as rudely as he did. He also remembered a conversation in which Rebecca revealed that she was under pressure from the company's senior team to demonstrate that she had fresh ideas. With these things in mind, he asked Rebecca out for coffee, explained that he wanted to maintain their relationship but that he was hurt by her behavior. At first, Rebecca was defen-

sive, claiming that it was all in Antonio's head, but when he gave a few examples, she conceded that she'd been stressed and was perhaps taking it out on him. He offered to support her in meetings, even brainstorming ideas with her beforehand, and she vowed to watch the interruptions. They continued to work together for five more years and relied on each other for candid feedback and advice.

You might be tempted to think that Celia was in a tougher situation than Antonio—she was dealing with a stubborn peer and an important client situation. She had the CEO breathing down her neck, too. But Celia's conflict wasn't any worse or more intense than Antonio's. He was dealing with his boss—the most influential person in his work life—and stood to lose a lot if things went south. Antonio simply handled the situation better. He took time to think through what was really happening, to see the conflict from Rebecca's perspective, and to prepare for his discussion with her.

Celia, of course, is not alone. When we perceive the risks of engaging in conflict to be greater than the potential upsides, many of us prefer to stifle our feelings and move on rather than speak up. And understandably so, as there are negative consequences to mishandling disagreements.

The Downsides of Conflict

Linda Hill's story in the preface and Celia's story here illustrate that when handled poorly—or avoided altogether—conflict can derail projects, damage client relationships, or lose company business. Initiatives slow to a standstill, while warring factions sort out their differences or teams risk not meeting their goals at all. "Energy and creativity get siphoned off," explains Annie McKee, an expert in emotional intelligence, and rather than focusing on accomplishing their objectives, team members are absorbed by their differences. And people in organizations, says McKee, "often have a very long memory when it comes to fighting at work. It doesn't matter what the underlying cause was or who was right or wrong. All people remember is that it was a mess, and that you were involved."

Avoiding conflict (as Celia chose to do) can just make things worse. In fact, unspoken disagreements can have consequences that are as significant as a conference room shouting match. Jeanne Brett, a negotiations professor, warns, "Conflict that's not expressed can be worse than conflict that is." Sometimes we're upset with people and they have no idea we're struggling with them. This negativity can bleed into your interactions. Or worse, your feelings simmer underneath the surface until your coworker does something that makes you explode, blindsiding your unsuspecting colleague.

Conflict also takes an emotional toll. "When you're consumed with a fight, it's hard to draw the boundary and it often spills over into your life," says McKee. We shred our nails worrying about what to say to a colleague with whom we're fighting, or we waste hours agonizing over whether we could have better articulated our perspective on a contentious issue. Over time, persistent conflict causes health problems. A Duke University Medical Center study showed that an intensely angry episode can lead to an eightfold increase in risk of heart attack, and anger has been linked to strokes, irregular heartbeat, sleep problems, excess eating, and insulin resistance, which can help cause diabetes.

The Benefits of Conflict

Luckily, however, when handled well, conflict can have positive outcomes: It can help you be more creative, spark new ideas, and even strengthen bonds with your coworkers, as it did between Antonio and Rebecca. You might dream of living in a peaceful utopia, but it wouldn't be good for your company, your work, or you. "Conflict allows the team to come to terms with difficult situations, to synthesize diverse perspectives, and to make sure solutions are well thought out. Conflict is uncomfortable, but it is the source of true innovation and also a critical process in identifying and mitigating risks," says Liane Davey, an expert in team dynamics.

Here are some of the specific benefits:

- **Better work outcomes:** When you and your coworkers push one another to continuously ask if there's a better approach, that creative friction is likely to lead to new solutions. And there's rarely a fixed amount of value to be gained in a disagreement. If you and your colleague are arguing about the best way to roll out a new initiative—he wants to launch in a single market first and you want to enter several at one time—you'll be forced to explore the pros and cons of each approach and ideally find the best solutions. It may be that you decide to run the pilot he wants but on a shorter time frame so that you get the revenue from reaching the other markets sooner.

- **Opportunity to learn and grow:** As uncomfortable as it may feel when someone challenges your ideas, it's an opportunity to learn. You gain experience from incorporating feedback, try new things, and evolve as a manager. When a peer chews you out after an important presentation because you didn't give her team credit for their work, the words may sting, but you're more likely to think through everyone's perspectives before preparing your next talk.

- **Improved relationships:** By working through conflict together, you'll feel closer to the people around you and gain a better understanding of what matters to them and how they prefer to work. You'll also set an important precedent: that it's possible to have "good" fights and then move on. Two regional managers who engage in a lengthy debate about who should be responsible for maintaining quality in their region have, at the end of the day, learned information about each other that will help them work better together in the future. And they've shown their teams that it's possible to move beyond conflict, to not get entrenched in a viewpoint but to make progress toward a resolution.

- **Job satisfaction:** When you're not afraid to constructively disagree, or even fight, about issues at work, you're likely to be happier to go to the office, be satisfied with what you accomplish, and enjoy interactions with your colleagues. Instead of feeling as if you have to walk on eggshells, you can focus on getting your work done. A study in China showed a correlation between the use of certain approaches to conflict management—ones in which employees pursue a win-win situation, care for others, and focus on common interests—and an employee's happiness at work.

For conflict to have any of these benefits, you have to learn the skills to proactively address problems and engage in healthy discussions. Fortunately, you have ample opportunity to try. The average person spends nearly three hours each week dealing with conflict at work, according to a study by CPP Global. Another study by CPP showed that managers report spending 18% to 26% of their time dealing with conflicts. Since we spend so much time engaged in disagreements, it's worth our effort to get them right—to temper our reactions and manage the conflict so that it's more productive.

How do you do that? This book will help you break through the scary, emotional stuff and take a practical, ordered approach to dealing with conflict.

A Plan for Handling Conflict

I'll briefly outline here a better approach for handling conflict so that you get a sense of the whole process before delving into the individual steps and specific scenarios in later chapters.

You start by understanding conflict better. Before we engage in an unhealthy way, it helps to know what's at the root of the disagreement. First, you need to know the various sources of conflict (see chapter 1, "Types of Conflict"). There are four main types: **relationship** (a personal disagreement), **task** (disagreement over what the goal is), **process** (disagreement over the means or process for achieving a goal), and **status** (disagreement over your standing in a group). These categories will help you figure out what's actually happening when you get into a conflict—even when your fight doesn't neatly fit into one bucket.

The second piece of information you need is to understand your options (see chapter 2, "Your Options for Handling Conflict"). In general, there are four from which to choose when confronting a conflict. The first, which is more common than you might think, is to **do nothing**. You don't say anything to your colleague, you let the comment go, or you simply walk away and go on as if the conflict hasn't happened. The second option is to address the conflict, but **indirectly**. Instead of talking through what's going on with your coworker, you might involve your boss or a third party, or hint at the conflict without ever candidly naming it. This option is more common in cultures such as East Asia, where saving face is important. The third option is to address the conflict **directly.** This is where the rest of the book focuses—on preparing for and having a direct conversation with your counterpart. The final option—and typically your last resort—is to **exit** the relationship.

The third and final aspect to having a more productive conflict is to know what people's natural tendencies are when it comes to conflict. There are generally two types of people: those who gravitate toward conflict and those who want to take cover under their desks whenever tensions rise. **Avoiders** tend to shy away or even hide from disagreements. **Seekers** are more eager to engage in conflict when it arises (or even find ways to create it). In chapter 3 ("Recognize Your Natural Tendency"), you'll get to know which style you gravitate toward (and tips for sussing out your counterpart's tendency) so that you can make a conscious choice about how to address a disagreement.

Table I-1 gives you an overview of this foundational work.

Once you've completed this groundwork, it's time to put your knowledge into practice. When faced with a specific situation—your colleague raises his voice, you're battling with your finance counterpart over next year's budget, your boss is acting like a jerk—start by quickly taking stock of what you know about your counterpart

TABLE I-1

Conflict at a glance

Types of conflict (conflict is over . . .)	Options for handling	Natural tendencies
1. **Relationship** (personal issues, such as how you're being treated)	1. **Do nothing.**	1. **Conflict avoider** • Shies away from disagreements • Cares most about harmony
2. **Task** (the goal, *what* you're trying to achieve)	2. **Address indirectly.**	
3. **Process** (the process, *how* work gets done)	3. **Address directly.**	2. **Conflict seeker** • Eager to engage in disagreements
4. **Status** (your standing in a group or who's in charge)	4. **Exit the relationship.**	• Cares most about directness and honesty

(is she a seeker like you, or are you both avoiders?) and the type of conflict you're having (see chapter 4, "Assess the Situation"). This will give you a better picture of what you're up against.

You'll also need to sort out what your goal is: Do you want to move your stalled project forward? Preserve the relationship? Just move on? That will help you make a smart choice about which of your four options to exercise. If you choose to do nothing or exit the relationship, this is where your journey ends. You can skip to chapter 8 ("Repair the Relationship") and focus on how to rebuild trust and move on. If you prefer to address the conflict indirectly, you'll choose one of the tactics laid out in chapter 4. If you decide to address the conflict directly, then you'll start to prepare for the conversation (see chapter 5, "Get Ready for the Conversation"). This involves the following eight steps:

1. Check your mindset.

2. See the situation from your counterpart's perspective.

3. Consider the larger organizational context.

4. Plan your message.

5. Prepare for multiple scenarios.

6. Pick the right time.

7. Choose the right place.

8. Vent.

Then you're ready to sit down with your colleague and talk through what's happening (see chapter 6, "Have a Productive Conversation"). You'll start by framing the conversation so that you get off on the right foot. You want to form a bond with your counterpart by focusing on where you agree. Then you'll do three things simultaneously: Manage your and your counterpart's emotions, listen to your colleague's perspective, and make your viewpoint heard. These are all toward the goal of trying to find a solution to the underlying conflict.

Ideally in that conversation, or in subsequent ones, you'll find a resolution that meets both of your needs (see chapter 7, "Get to a Resolution and Make a Plan"). And if you aren't able to reach a conclusion, you'll at least agree on how to move forward.

No matter what sort of end your conflict comes to, you'll need to figure out how to repair the relationship and move on (see chapter 8). Conflict can bring up lots of negative emotions—anger, frustration, annoyance, resentment—and it's important to clear the air and lay the groundwork for a strong relationship going forward.

Conflict can feel less scary and more manageable when you approach it methodically. You'll need to be flexible and adapt as the situation takes unexpected turns, but this book will help you develop the basic skills and strategies you need. There are many examples throughout (real stories disguised and combined) to show you how others have tackled similar challenges. Of course, nothing ever goes exactly as planned, so the final chapter addresses specific scenarios, such as what to do when you're dealing with a bully or how to navigate a disagreement with a vendor (see chapter 9, "Navigate Common Situations"). When you learn to manage conflict, it has fewer downsides and more benefits, and it boosts your overall productivity. "If you're going to be a truly effective manager, you're going to have to deal with conflict. Otherwise you're going to end up fighting with everyone or simply giving them what they want," says John Ratey, a professor of psychiatry at Harvard Medical School. By following the process in this guide, you can reap the benefits of conflict while mitigating its risks. You will also become more confident in proactively addressing disagreements and engaging in difficult discussions.

SECTION ONE

Preparing for Conflict Before It Happens

CHAPTER 1

Types of Conflict

In the middle of a dispute, when your brain kicks into overdrive, you might be stuck wondering, Where did this conversation go wrong? or Why is my coworker so mad? It might feel as if your colleague is being unreasonable, that the situation is intractable, or that your relationship will never recover.

Uncovering what's truly going on—what's at the root of the disagreement—will help you set aside your emotional reaction and begin to solve the problem.

There are generally four types of conflict: relationship, task, process, and status (see table 1-1).

The common sources of conflict are neatly delineated here, but in reality, disagreements rarely fall into just one of these categories. More often, there are multiple things going on and a conflict may start as one type and expand into another. We'll follow the story of a cross-functional team at TechCorp, a fictional tech company, to illustrate what these categories look like in the real world.

TABLE 1-1

Types of conflict

Type of conflict	What it is	For example . . .	Outcomes if you get it right
Relationship	A clash of personalities	Your counterpart interrupts and talks over you in a meeting.	• Better understanding of your counterpart • Improved relationship
Task	A disagreement over the intended goal of a task or project	You and your colleague in the legal department don't agree on how much risk the company should assume in a partnership agreement.	• Clearer understanding of the trade-offs to be made • Better results • Innovation
Process	A disagreement over how to carry out a project or task	You think it's important to roll out a new initiative quickly, even if it means sacrificing some quality, while your counterpart believes it needs to be perfect before it hits the market.	• Process innovation • More potential solutions to the problem
Status	A disagreement over who's in charge or gets credit for the work	You and your peer are competing to run a high-profile project.	• Clear hierarchy • Easier coordination of the work

Relationship

This is what we most often assume is happening when we get into a conflict—a clash of personalities.

What it is

A personal disagreement. Sometimes called an interpersonal or emotional conflict, it's when one or both of you feel disrespected or hurt. It includes:

- Snapping at each other in meetings

- Exchanging snarky emails

- Avoiding eye contact in the hallway

- Interrupting, or talking over, a colleague in a meeting

- Using a condescending tone to indicate your disagreement

- Arguing over who's right and who's wrong

Quite often a relationship conflict starts as something else. A disagreement over a project schedule escalates to bickering that disrupts a team meeting. Or a difference of opinion on the company's strategy devolves into a heated debate about who's right and who's wrong. You may both have valid points, and good intentions, but some disagreements turn ugly. Annie McKee describes it this way: "In a perfect world, we follow the textbook advice, treat conflict logically, behave like adults, and get on with it. The problem is, we're not working in a perfect world, and none of us is perfect. We each bring our own baggage to work every day. And some of our issues—insecurity, the desire for power and control, habitual victimhood—rear their heads again and again."

Example

A team of functional leaders at TechCorp all agree that one of their best-performing products needs a new feature, but the SVP of product development and the SVP of engineering can't agree on the ultimate goal. Their differing views gradually escalated from lively debate to a public blowout. Now they trade passive-aggressive barbs over group emails and interrupt each other in meetings. Some teammates have become so uncomfortable witnessing the interactions that they've started declining meetings in which they know both will be present. Not only do the SVPs disagree, they can't believe that the other person doesn't see it the same way. It's no longer about what's best for TechCorp and the customer. For both of them, it's about being right.

The benefits of managing it well

There are typically few benefits to relationship conflict, says Jeanne Brett. When our egos and sense of pride get involved, it's painful, and challenging to manage effectively.

But even uncomfortable interpersonal conflict can have positive outcomes. Jonathan Hughes, an expert on corporate negotiations and relationship management, points out that these types of disputes give us the opportunity to learn more about ourselves and our colleagues. We better understand each other's values, working styles, and personalities and therefore build better relationships, "which creates a virtuous cycle," he says. If you've established that you can successfully navigate conflict, you're more likely to give honest feedback and challenge each other when necessary.

Task

The most common source of disagreement at work is task conflict.

What it is

A dispute over the goal of a task or project or what you're trying to achieve. This includes disagreements about:

- The agenda for a staff meeting

- How the success of a new initiative should be defined or measured

- Whether the customers or the employees should come first

- How much risk a company should assume when partnering with other organizations

- Whether to prioritize revenue or customer satisfaction

"The most common form of task conflict in organizations is functional," explains Brett. Marketing, legal, and finance may look at the same problem and see it completely differently. For example, marketing may lobby to put the customer first, while legal's aim is to protect the company from risk, and finance is trying to cut costs. Each may argue that their perspective on how to solve the problem is more important. "In reality, all those viewpoints and each functional way of addressing the problem are relevant and should be integrated into the solution," says Brett.

Example

The functional leaders at TechCorp all agree that they want the new feature, but they can't agree on the objective. Marketing sees it as an opportunity to expand the company's market share. Finance is focused on improving the business's margins. And the engineers on the team care about developing something cool that integrates the latest technology. If they can't agree on what success means for the new feature, they won't be able to move the project forward—or even worse, they'll each take it in a separate direction, wasting time and the company's resources. The engineers spent all weekend developing a prototype of the new feature, but the finance managers are worried that it will be too expensive to produce and the marketing lead isn't sure users will appreciate the added functionality.

The benefits of managing it well

When we have productive discussions about our different views of project goals or how we should define success, we gain valuable insights, says Hughes. "We live in a world of finite resources, and this type of conversation is helpful in terms of coming to smart decisions about which trade-offs to make." Should the new feature have less functionality and be more affordable to make? Or is it important to delight customers so that they stay with the company longer? At TechCorp, the new feature is likely to be more robust and useful to the customer precisely because each of the functions is pushing its own agenda. The new feature won't satisfy everyone, but airing each group's goals is likely to serve up new ideas and generate productive conversations about what will make the feature successful—more so than if the team had just driven toward one person's objective.

Process

Another common type of conflict is not about *what* you're doing but *how* you're doing it.

What it is

A disagreement over how to carry out a project or task, the means or process you use to reach your goal. This includes differences on:

- The best tactic for reaching a quarterly target

- How to implement a new HR policy

- How decisions should be made in a meeting

- How quickly a project should be completed

- Who should be consulted and included as the project is carried out

Process disagreements are easily confused with task conflicts. You think you're arguing over the outcome when really you can't agree on how to make a decision.

For example, you might get locked into a battle with a coworker over the right strategy for a new project when what you need to settle is not the specific tactic but who gets to make the final call. Or you think the company should do customer research first and a coworker thinks it should get a good-enough product out in the market and see what happens.

Example

At TechCorp, finance thinks that the group should come up with a proposal for the new feature that everyone can agree on, but marketing is lobbying to take a vote and let the majority rule. Marketing is also at odds with the engineers because they think they should conduct customer focus groups throughout the course of development, starting as soon as possible, while the engineers think they should wait until they have an internally approved prototype. None of the three functions agrees on the timeline for completing the project—in time for an important trade show or within the fiscal year.

The benefits of managing it well

Disagreements over how to get something done can help bring about process improvements or unearth hidden benefits. A good way to come up with several viable options, Hughes suggests, is to ask, "What other ways can we imagine meeting our goals?" and then allow your team to offer answers. "People tend to frame things in an unnecessary binary fashion: should we do this or that, but there's almost always a third or fourth way as well," he says. It's natural for finance to lobby for production schedules that align with fiscal year milestones. But discussing the timing with the entire group reveals a critical trade show date, reminds the group of key fiscal-year dates, and allows everyone to share their own team's schedule and resource constraints. As with task conflict, process conflict can improve results by drawing on the expertise of the whole group.

Status

A less common—but still problematic—source of conflict is when people disagree over their standing within a group.

What it is

A disagreement over who's in charge or who deserves credit for the work. For example, you think you should be leading an initiative, while your worker thinks he should. It can also include:

- Jockeying for leadership, especially in a team without a formal or designated leader

- Competing to run a high-profile project

- Arguing over or dominating shared resources

- Competing for status symbols, such as the corner office, the latest technology, or having an administrative assistant

Example

The SVP of engineering at TechCorp and the SVP of new product development are going head to head over which one of them should lead the group that's designing the new feature. In an effort to gain an advantage in this horse race, when the senior leaders congratulate the team on the work so far, the SVP of engineering credits the long hours his group put in, while the SVP of new product development claims it was her team's brainstorming sessions and market research that led to the concept for the snazzy new feature.

The benefits of managing it well

When a status conflict is resolved, there's clarity for the team and anyone working with them. "A clear status hierarchy is efficient in that everyone knows his or her role and responsibility," says Brett. This makes it easier to coordinate work and get things done smoothly. "In stable social hierarchies, lower-status individuals defer to those with higher status, and higher-status individuals look out for the welfare of lower-status ones. At least that is how it is supposed to work," she says.

It bears repeating that it's rare to have a conflict that fits neatly into just one of these categories. Often, as the TechCorp example shows, disagreements have elements of all four, and many that start as another type end up as relationship conflicts. Separating out each type cuts through the noise of the conflict to what's really at hand. Instead of a morass of disagreements, you have an organized list of issues to resolve. "Finding the root causes helps you get into problem-solving mode," says Hughes. "It doesn't automatically solve everything. It's not like the heavens open and the angels sing and the conflict is over. But it does make it easier to resolve."

No matter what kind of conflict you're having—or if your conflict is a mess of all four types—you aren't stuck. You have options for moving forward.

CHAPTER 2

Your Options for Handling Conflict

Some people might tell you that the only way to manage work disagreements is to dive right in and straighten things out. This isn't true. While dealing with the conflict directly can be the most effective route, it isn't the only one.

In this chapter I explain your four options: Do nothing, address it indirectly, address it directly, and exit the relationship (see table 4-2 in chapter 4, "Assess the Situation," for an overview of these options).

Do Nothing

When you choose to do nothing, you don't say anything to your colleague, you let the comment go, or you simply walk away and carry on as if the conflict didn't happen. Instead of acting on any feelings or impulses you have about a disagreement, you swallow them and move on. This isn't a cop-out—it's a seemingly easy and low-effort option for managing conflict. "Most people tend toward loyalty," says Brian Uzzi, a leadership professor. "That's because it's easier to lower your expectations than deal with the real issues at hand." To be clear, this isn't taking your bat and ball and going home or storming off. This is simply keeping an issue to yourself rather than raising it.

We do this all the time, often without realizing it. "We put up with an awful lot on a day-to-day basis. We lump conflict all the time without consciously making a decision to do so," says Jeanne Brett. For many conflicts, it's a perfectly good approach. It can be a smart move, especially if the risks of addressing the issue feel greater than the potential rewards. "There are certain discussions you're just better off not having at all, and knowing when to let it go is just as critical as knowing when to engage," she says. (For more on making that call, see chapter 4, "Assess the Situation.")

It may not be worth having the conversation if you don't think it's going to go anywhere. "If your colleague is stuck in her ways and has never demonstrated a willingness to concede, what do you gain by pushing her yet again? If the damage is already done—say the project was defunded last week and you're just finding out about it—it's probably better to forget about it and move on," says Brett.

The risk in selecting this option is that your resolve may not stick. The issue may not go away, so your feelings about it may come out sideways as you blow up at your colleague about an unrelated matter. Or your colleague's behavior may continue or worsen because he is unaware of the problem.

Note that this option and the "address it indirectly" option are different than avoiding conflict altogether. Conflict avoidance is a natural tendency to steer away from conflict whenever possible (see chapter 3, "Recognize Your Natural Tendency"). These are active, conscious decisions you make to handle a situation. If you tend to avoid conflict, check yourself if you find that you gravitate toward these two options.

Use when . . .

- You don't have the energy or time to invest in preparing for and having a conversation

- You suspect the other person is unwilling to have a constructive conversation

- You have little or no power, particularly in conflicts with people above you

- You won't beat yourself up or stew about it

Keep in mind that this option . . .

- Requires little work on your part, but it can be frustrating to dismiss your feelings

- Keeps the relationship stable, assuming you can both truly move on

- Won't work if you're unable to put it behind you and you risk having an outburst later or acting passive-aggressively toward your counterpart

- May cause your work to suffer if you continue to feel bad

- Can reinforce bad behavior—if your counterpart got away with it once, she might try again

What it looks like in practice

Clara, a project manager, was helping Lisa, a product manager, develop a launch schedule for testing a new product line, and she thought that Lisa was being overly optimistic. She tried to point out that Lisa's dates weren't realistic, but Lisa wouldn't listen. "I was new, and while her time frame seemed aggressive to me, I couldn't be sure," Clara says. "Plus she isn't the warmest person, and she made it clear she wasn't really open to my feedback." When the plan went to the wider team, things blew up. The production manager couldn't believe that Clara thought her team would drop everything to meet her dates. But Lisa had already shared the schedule with the head of marketing, who had announced the launch date in the market. When the team discussed the schedule, Lisa never once explained that Clara had a difference of opinion and, in fact, implied that the dates were Clara's work.

"I was livid," explains Clara, "but I didn't want to get into a fight in front of our bosses." She later explained the situation to her manager but decided not to talk with Lisa about it. "She didn't strike me as the kind of person who would be interested in hashing it out, and this wasn't the last time we'd have to work together," she says. "I didn't see what good would come of it, other than creating more tension." Instead, she put it behind her and continued to work with Lisa. Though they never directly discussed the issue, Clara says that Lisa was more open to her input on schedules in the future.

Address It Indirectly: Skirt the Issue

If you decide to try to change the situation by addressing it, there are two ways to do that. The first is to confront someone indirectly.

Indirect confrontation is when you choose to circle around an issue rather than naming it and addressing it together. Maybe you appeal to someone else who can talk to your counterpart (say, your boss or a coworker who knows the person better), or you talk about the situation without ever naming the issue. To those in certain cultures that tend to address conflict directly, this may sound backhanded and completely ineffective. But in some places, particularly those where saving face is important, this is the approach of choice. "In many Asian cultures, group harmony is incredibly important. It's not appropriate to say, 'We have a disagreement,'" says Erin Meyer, author of *The Culture Map: Breaking Through the Invisible Boundaries of Global Business.* "If you have a conflict with someone on a Japanese team, for example, you would not sit down and talk it through."

Brett explains that one tactic is to use a story or a metaphor. For example, if you're upset about a colleague who is constantly interrupting you, you might tell a story about an employee you previously managed who struggled to listen. The moral of the story—that listening is a valuable but tough-to-learn skill—may prompt your counterpart to reflect on her own behavior. "You see this all the time in China and other Asian countries. They are respecting the other party to understand the problem and do something about it rather than telling them what to do," says Brett.

Another way to indirectly address a conflict is to get a third party involved. "In some African cultures, when you have a conflict, you work through a friend. That person works it out for you so that you never have a direct confrontation," says Meyer. You might go to your boss and explain that your interrupting colleague is preventing you from conducting a successful meeting. In some cultures it may be clear that you expect that she will talk to your coworker. In others, you may need to ask. Similarly, if you and another team member don't agree on how to spend money in your shared budget, you might ask your boss to make the decision so that neither of you is seen as losing. Instead, you're just carrying out your manager's orders. Again, in Western cultures, this might be frowned upon because you may be seen as giving away your power or failing to step up to the plate, but in other places, this is an effective way to handle the disagreement.

This option has several risks. If your indirect approach is too indirect, your counterpart may completely miss the message you're trying to send and may not change, or he may just think that "someone else" really messed up. Another risk is that your counterpart hears that you were reaching out to other people about his behavior and may resent that you went around him rather than speaking with him about it first. Lastly, if your counterpart is from a more direct culture, he may not respect what he perceives to be a passive approach.

Remember that this option and the "do nothing" option are different than avoiding conflict altogether. Steering away from conflict is not the same as making a conscious choice to address it indirectly. Watch out if you tend to avoid conflict and find yourself exercising this option regularly.

Use when . . .

- It's important in your culture to save face and not embarrass people

- You work in a place (office or country) where direct confrontation is inappropriate

- You think the other person will be more willing to take feedback from someone else—either someone more powerful than you, such as a boss, or someone he trusts, such as a close confidant

Keep in mind that this option . . .

- May not work in Western cultures, where the expectation is generally to speak directly with someone when you have a problem

- Can backfire if your counterpart finds out about your behind-the-scenes work and is unhappy about it

- May fail if your counterpart doesn't understand your story or metaphor

What it looks like in practice

Carlos worked as an estimator for a large contractor company, and his new boss, Peter, was a classic micromanager.

"He was very operations focused and wanted to know what I was doing all the time," says Carlos. "I was constantly getting emails from him asking about details on my projects that he didn't need to know." Carlos was afraid that if he told Peter he was micromanaging him, Peter would get worse, not trusting that Carlos would do the work the way Peter wanted. "I was good at my job. I just needed him to back off some," explains Carlos.

He decided to approach the conversation by talking to Peter about one of his own direct reports, Vince. "I told him that since Vince was new, he probably needed some closer managing, but that I really saw our job as helping these younger people to learn the job on their own and empower them as much as possible," he says. Peter was a bit hesitant and tried to argue that some people needed to be micromanaged. The two then got into a discussion about who needed closer supervision and who didn't. Without addressing the issue directly, Carlos was able to make the case that he didn't need Peter always looking over his shoulder. And it worked. Peter still managed Carlos more closely than Carlos preferred, but the conversation seemed to encourage Peter to give Carlos a longer leash.

Address It Directly: Confront the Issue

You can also try to change the situation by explicitly addressing it. A direct confrontation is when you talk to the other person—either in the moment the conflict arises or at a later time. Generally this involves explaining your side of the conflict, listening to the other person's perspective, and then, ideally, agreeing on a resolution.

For those in more assertive cultures such as the United States, this can be an effective option, and it's the one I focus on for most of this book. Meyer also points to other countries, such as France, Russia, and Spain, where it's acceptable to have "open, vigorous, strong" disagreements. Some organizational cultures are also more prone to addressing conflict directly, says Brett. The financial industry, for example, has a reputation for people openly disagreeing, sometimes in seemingly harsh ways.

This can be a risky option if it's not handled well because it might heighten the conflict rather than defuse it. That's why the majority of this book is dedicated to showing you how to prepare for the conversation, engage productively, and reach a resolution.

Use when . . .

- You worry that there will be lingering resentment if you don't clear the air

- You've tried to do nothing or indirectly address it and the problem persists

- You previously had a positive relationship with the person and you want to get it back on track

Keep in mind that this option . . .

- Can be good for a relationship—going through difficult experiences together can make your connection stronger and your relationship more resilient

- Allows you to voice your opinion or feelings, if that's important to you

- Helps you develop a better understanding of yourself and your counterpart

- Can improve your work if you can incorporate others' views and opinions

- Could earn you a reputation as aggressive or combative if you do it too often (or not well)

What it looks like in practice

A close work friend of Aparna's pulled her aside to tell her that another coworker of theirs, Zia, had been spreading rumors that Aparna was looking for a new job. Aparna knew that Zia was competitive with her—their jobs were closely related—and that in Zia's ideal world, she would take over several of Aparna's projects. But Aparna was not on the job market. "It was absurd. I hadn't had one networking conversation, and I'd barely updated my résumé in years," she says. She and Zia had small disagreements in the past over what direction to take particular projects, but they'd always been able to move past them. "I always thought we were healthy competitors. We made each other work harder."

Worried that Zia's rumors would put her position at risk, especially if her boss heard them, she decided to talk with Zia directly. She asked Zia out for coffee and explained what she heard and asked for her perspective on it. At first Zia denied that she had said anything to anyone, but she eventually conceded that she'd heard something about Aparna talking with a competitor and she may have mentioned it to a few people. Aparna explained that that was not the case and asked Zia to stop. She agreed, and while they continued to compete on occasion, Aparna didn't hear news of Zia talking behind her back again.

Exit: Get Out of the Situation Entirely

Your final option is to extricate yourself from the situation by either getting reassigned to another project, finding a new boss, or leaving the company. This is usually a last resort. "You can't always leave a relationship, especially at work," Uzzi says. When you're disagreeing with a boss or someone on your team, you may just be stuck with that person, unless you're willing to find another job. But if the conflict is with someone in another department or a person outside your company, such as a vendor, you may be able to reduce your contact.

Exiting doesn't mean that you end the relationship by making a dramatic scene. Instead, look for a way to stop interacting with that person. If it's a client with whom you have an ongoing conflict, you may explain the situation to your supervisor and propose that one of your equally qualified colleagues replaces you on the account. If it's someone you work with in the finance department, you can begin to build a relationship with someone else on that team so that you have an alternative contact. If your boss is the problem, you might apply to jobs in other departments; you can start by building a broader network in the organization or connecting with people on teams you may want to join.

This sounds easier said than done, and often it is. Exiting is a risky option because it's not something you can typically do overnight or even in a week's time. More likely it's something you'll build toward slowly, while you dust off your résumé, expand your network, and have conversations with people who may be able to support you in making the move.

Brett says that it's usually worth trying the other three options before ending things completely. But there are situations in which the conflict is so bad and seemingly intractable that severing the relationship is the best option.

Use when . . .

- You're dealing with someone from another department or outside your company where your jobs aren't interdependent

- You can easily find another job somewhere else

- You've tried other options and nothing has worked

Keep in mind that this option . . .

- May give you a sense of relief because it gives you a clean break

- Can protect you from further time wasted, stress, and discomfort

- Is likely to take a lot of work from you (including potentially difficult conversations) to change departments, get reassigned, or leave your job

- May hurt other relationships as you sever ties with this person

- Can have negative repercussions if you leave a project and then you're later blamed for its failure because you abandoned the team or client

- May make *you* seem as though you're difficult to work with

What it looks like in practice

When the 50-person department that Monique worked in was restructured, she wasn't happy with her new direct supervisor, Samir. "He didn't know how to manage. He was patronizing. He didn't seem interested in my contributions. And it wasn't clear what he wanted me to be doing," she explains. To make matters worse, she didn't believe in the direction Samir was taking the department, a unit that she had spent years helping to build. She repeatedly tried to get clearer directions from him, but the conversations quickly disintegrated, leaving Monique frustrated and Samir confused. "It felt near impossible to have a constructive conversation with him," she says.

After six months of pulling her hair out, Monique went to the head of HR, with whom she had a positive relationship. She didn't want to complain openly for fear that it would get back to her boss. "That would've felt like tattle telling. Instead, I explained to her that as Samir's responsibilities were expanding, he probably had more than enough to do," she says. She suggested that maybe she could report to a different manager. "She thought it was an interesting idea," she says. A couple of weeks went by, and during one of her one-on-one meetings with Samir, he proposed the new reporting structure and asked how she felt about it. Her response, "Whatever's best for the team, I'm willing to do." Monique was very happy with her new manager and felt she had done the best she could do under the circumstances. "If things hadn't changed, I would've left the company," she says.

When Your Counterpart Takes the Lead

Sometimes you're not the one who gets to decide which option to pursue. Your counterpart may ask to be taken off your project. Or a colleague may start yelling at you in the hallway after a meeting. "If it's the other party who's having the problem, you may not be able to completely avoid having the conversation," says Brett. If you're put on the spot, try to delay the conversation for when you're in a better frame of mind so that you can make a smart choice about the option that will work best. (See chapter 4 for more on walking away from a conflict.)

Here are a few examples of language you could use to put off a fight with someone who's upset:

- "I understand you want to discuss this, but now isn't the best time. Can we schedule something at a later date so that we can talk it through?"

- "I can see you're really upset about this. Can we talk about this when we're both calmer?"

- "I'm not ready to have this conversation right now. I'm going to step outside to clear my head, and then perhaps we can meet tomorrow to talk about this."

If your counterpart makes the first move, then you must choose how to react. Your options are the same, but it would be hard for you to do nothing, for example, if he's requested that you sit down and talk about an issue. And you certainly won't need to exercise your right to exit if he's already done so.

Whether you're choosing an approach or whether your counterpart initiates a difficult conversation, there's work for you to do. You'll have to deal with your anger or hurt if you elect to do nothing, finagle a new position or job if you decide to exit the relationship, make a careful plan if you decide to address it indirectly, or prepare for a difficult conversation if you decide to address it directly. That work will be easier if you understand the two general approaches to conflict and which one you tend to favor.

CHAPTER 3

Recognize Your Natural Tendency

There are generally two types of people: those who avoid conflict and those who seek it. Neither style is better or worse, so instead of beating yourself up for being resistant to conflict or being drawn to it, accept that you have a default approach, says Amy Jen Su, an executive coach. Knowing which style is your (and eventually your counterpart's) natural tendency allows you to make smart choices about how to address the conflict and, if you decide to confront it, have a constructive conversation.

Of course, it's rare for a person to avoid conflict or seek it out all of the time. It's more likely that you adjust your style based on the context (are you at home or at work?); whom you're having the conflict with (your boss or your direct report?); and other things going on (is the organization under extensive scrutiny from investors; are you feeling particularly stressed-out, or did you just return

TABLE 3-1

Conflict styles at a glance

Avoiders	Seekers
• Shy away from disagreements. • Value harmony and positive relationships. • Often try to placate people or change the topic. • Don't want to hurt others' feelings. • Don't want to disrupt team dynamics.	• Are eager to engage in disagreements. • Care most about directness and honesty. • Strongly advocate for their own perspective. • Lose patience when people aren't being direct or honest. • Don't mind ruffling feathers.

from a rejuvenating vacation?). You might be willing to tell your sister that she's out of line, but you'd probably tone down a similar comment when you're directing it at a colleague. "This may be because we're more mindful with some audiences than others. With a customer you're trying to sell to, you might be more avoidant [of conflict]. With a peer you've worked with for years, you might be a seeker," says Jen Su.

Still, knowing which style you gravitate toward will help you make a conscious choice about how to address a disagreement. If you're an avoider, for example, your instinct may be to do nothing. But knowing that's your natural tendency can help you overcome your resistance to addressing issues. See table 3-1 for an overview of the characteristics of each. The following sections offer more detail to help you identify your most common approach.

Conflict Avoiders

Conflict avoiders are generally people who value harmony in the workplace. When they sense a disagreement brewing, they will often try to placate the other person or change the topic. These aren't passive behaviors, but active things they do to prevent conflict from becoming an issue. They believe having positive relationships with their colleagues is extremely important and are often seen as easy to get along with. Liane Davey describes these people this way: "They worry that disagreeing might hurt someone's feelings or disrupt harmonious team dynamics. They fret that their perspective isn't as valid as someone else's, so they hold back."

This strategy is meant to make things easier, but it can take a toll. Conflict avoiders try to be nice and often avoid contentious topics. But "[these people] end up spending an inordinate amount of time talking to themselves or others—complaining, feeling frustrated, ruminating on something that already happened, or anticipating something that might happen," says Jen Su. This avoidance can have physical manifestations as well. Some of Jen Su's more conflict-avoidant clients have experienced headaches, back pain, and weight gain.

If you're a conflict avoider, here are some examples of how you might think:

> "My colleague interrupted me again. We're supposed to be leading this effort together, and this is his way of showing he's the boss. He just makes me look bad in front of the team. I've been replaying it in my mind over and over again."

> "Someone has to tell my direct report that her bad attitude is affecting the rest of the team, but I'm

dreading it. I've been thinking about it all day and haven't been able to get anything done."

"I know what they're going to say—that we can't have more resources due to budget constraints. This gives me such a knot in my stomach. I'll probably just give up on asking for this investment."

"If I can just keep a smile on my face at the meeting, people will understand that I don't want to talk about the bugs that came up last week."

Conflict Seekers

Conversely, conflict seekers will seize on brewing disputes and amplify them, often strongly advocating for their perspective. They don't have patience when they think people aren't being direct or honest, and they're willing to ruffle a few feathers. The tendency to dive into conflict may feed upon itself because of a neurochemical process, as Judith E. Glaser, a communications expert, explains: "When you argue and win, your brain floods with different hormones—adrenaline and dopamine—which make you feel good, dominant, even invincible. It's a feeling any of us would want to replicate. So the next time we're in a tense situation, we fight again."

This attraction to conflict also takes a toll, but often on others. "Seekers are extremely good at fighting for their point of view (which may or may not be right), yet they are completely unaware of the dampening effect their behavior has on the people around them. If one person is getting high off his dominance, others are being drummed into submission," says Glaser.

Although it may not negatively affect them in the moment, their effectiveness as leaders and colleagues suffers. Though they "win" the argument, conflict seekers may earn the reputation of being difficult to work with, quick to snap, or even mean. People may avoid working with them or even describe them as bullies.

If you're a conflict seeker, here are some examples of how you might think:

"I can tell that many of them don't agree that we need to go with this vendor. But I know this is the right choice, even if they don't realize it yet."

"Why can't we get into this right now? Everyone should just lay out what they think the new strategy should be, and then we'll choose the best option. Why are we being so nice?"

"I couldn't believe my direct report had the nerve to question the deadline I laid out for the team. I was sure to shut her down and copied the others so that they all know in the future not to cross that line."

"Sal's recommendation on this hiring issue is just plain stupid. I owed it to him to tell him when he tried to get me on board with the new policy."

Identify Yourself

After reading the descriptions above, you may immediately recognize yourself as an avoider or a seeker. If it's not clear to you, taking the time to get to know yourself better is worthwhile. If a conflict erupts with your boss, you're not going to run home to take a personality test or soul search about your personal relationship to conflict. You won't have time for that. Knowing your preferred approach before you get into a heated debate can help you be better prepared for a discussion when the time comes.

To better understand what your natural tendency is, look at the many factors that contribute to your default approach:

- **Past experience:** "Our relationship to conflict is anchored in a history of habit," says Jen Su. If you were shamed or criticized during a conflict early in your career, you might choose safety and harmony over speaking up, she says. Or perhaps your first mentor enjoyed sparring with coworkers, demonstrating that there was nothing to fear. Maybe you're from a large family, who thrived on lively dinner table debates, so you frequently adopt the role of devil's advocate to spark heated team discussions.

- **Cultural norms:** Brett makes it clear: "You confront based on the norm in your culture." As discussed in the previous chapter, in East Asian cultures, for example, it's common to use an indirect approach. Others are typically more direct, such as Latin American cultures. This doesn't mean that every Chinese manager is a conflict avoider or that every Mexican manager is a conflict seeker; it's just another factor.

- **Office context:** Every workplace has its own set of
  norms, and some teams have their own separate
  set of rules as well. In some offices, it's frowned
  upon to disagree openly; you're expected to resolve
  disagreements in private meetings or through
  email. In other offices, it's common to have a more
  open airing of conflict.

- **Gender norms:** There's a stereotype that most
  women are conflict avoiders and most men are
  conflict seekers, which stems from the view that
  women are more nurturing and care more about
  what others think, say Amy Jen Su and her coauthor Muriel Maignan Wilkins in their book, *Own
  the Room: Discover Your Signature Voice to Master
  Your Leadership Presence.* But in practice this isn't
  necessarily true. Some women may opt to take
  less direct approaches to conflict because they
  know they will be penalized for being assertive. In
  fact, researchers at Harvard Business School and
  Babson College have shown that when women
  negotiate, people (both men and women) are less
  likely to want to work with them. So some women
  may lean toward being avoiders not because it's
  their natural tendency but because they know the
  social costs of being a conflict seeker are higher
  for them.

If you're still not sure which camp you fall into, here
are several tips for unearthing your preference.

Develop healthy self-awareness

Ask yourself some of the following questions about your current and previous relationship with conflict.

- Were you always more of a fighter? Or did you tend to accommodate others?

- Look back over particular moments of conflict early in your life or career—were you rewarded or punished for your approach?

- When you think about conflict now, do you get a pit in your stomach and feel like fleeing?

- Or does your heart race and you feel the urge to jump in?

- The last time tensions got high with someone at work or at home, how did you react?

- When you were growing up, how was conflict handled in your family?

- Do you come from a culture where conflict is handled more directly or one where it's frowned upon?

- What is the norm in your organization? In your unit? On your team? Do you adopt the typical approach or play against type?

Look for patterns in your answers. Perhaps you had always been a seeker until you were criticized as being "too aggressive" in an early performance review. Or maybe you notice that you tend to avoid conflict unless the issue is something you really care about, such as your team. You may be able to understand your tendency just by answering these questions. But it's also helpful to get more input.

Ask for feedback

It's tough to see ourselves for who we really are, so ask others to reality check your observations. Get feedback from trusted colleagues, a caring mentor, or even your spouse. Inquire specifically about conflict situations: "Do you see me as someone who backs away from disagreement? Or do I enjoy digging into an argument?" Jen Su warns that conflict seekers need to say explicitly that they want genuine and honest input. "More-aggressive people tend not to get the tough feedback they need because their colleagues are often afraid of them and don't want to trigger them." It's important, therefore, to ask someone who you know will be candid with you, perhaps someone who has little to lose in telling you the truth.

Take an assessment

Many of the psychometric tests that people use in the workplace, such as Myers-Briggs Type Indicator (MBTI), help you better understand how you handle conflict. However, there's one tool that's focused specifically on understanding your conflict style: the Thomas-Kilmann Conflict Mode Instrument (TKI). The tool categorizes you as having one of five conflict-handling styles— avoiding, accommodating, compromising, collaborating,

or competing—based on your answers to several questions. It's not time intensive (it usually takes about 15
minutes to complete), but there is a fee.

Reflecting on your approach is only half the battle; you
also need to get a sense of how your counterpart prefers
to approach disagreements before you can have a productive conflict.

Managing a Conflict

CHAPTER 4

Assess the Situation

When you're faced with a specific situation, there are five things to do to assess the scenario at hand before taking action—understand your counterpart; identify the type of conflict you're facing; consider the organizational context; determine your goal; and, finally, pick one of the four options you'll take to deal with this particular situation.

The first time you analyze a conflict using these five steps it will take some time, but eventually the analysis will get easier. The goal is to be able to quickly do these steps in your head whenever a disagreement arises.

Understand Your Counterpart

First, consider whom you're dealing with. Is he a conflict seeker or avoider? How does he typically communicate and how does he prefer to be communicated with? Is he more of a straight shooter who says things like they are or does he tend to beat around the bush? If you frequently work with the person you're in conflict with, you may already be familiar with his style. If you rarely interact with the person, you'll have to do some digging. "More and more we're working with people whom we don't have the luxury of getting that kind of intelligence on," says Amy Jen Su. It may be that you're fighting with an overseas colleague whom you see in person only at annual meetings, or your conflict is with a manager in a different department who sits in another building. "It's better to know something about the person rather than fighting in a vacuum," Jen Su says. She suggests that you get whatever information is available. Here's how.

Look for patterns

Whether or not you know your counterpart well, play the role of observer. How does she handle a tense discussion in a meeting? What's the look on her face when other people are disagreeing? Does she like people to cut to the chase and lay out just the facts or does she want the complete picture with every gory detail? What have you observed about her communication style? Look for patterns in how she communicates and clues in her behavior. "People who are volatile and confrontational, for example, tend to be that way in a lot of different situations," says Brett. Ideally you'll observe the person over time in multiple scenarios. That may not be possible, so take what you can get. Just keep in mind that the fewer instances you see, the less likely you'll be able to deduce an accurate pattern.

Get input from others

In addition to examining your counterpart's behavior, you might ask a colleague or two for input. Don't go around grilling others about him, but ask people to confirm or deny your observations. Say something like, "I noticed Jim flew off the handle in that meeting. Is that typical?" or "I saw Katerina avoid engaging with Tomas when he questioned whether her figures were right. Did you see the same thing?" You can also ask more direct questions: "Can you tell me how this person typically navigates conflict?" Obviously, you have to trust the person you're asking—you don't want your colleague to find out you're snooping on him.

Use this same approach to figure out cultural and office norms. If you're dealing with a vendor based in a different country, for example, or a colleague who's located halfway around the world, ask someone who knows that person or is familiar with the culture or office environment how conflict is typically handled. Erin Meyer suggests saying something along these lines: "Here's how I would deal with this in my culture. How would you typically approach it?" She also recommends that you seek out "cultural bridges," people who work in your culture and in your counterpart's. These are often ex-pats who've relocated to another office or people based out of headquarters who have to work across multiple locations.

Ask directly

It's not always advisable to come out and ask: "How do you like to address conflict?" That can be awkward—few people will be prepared to answer this question. Instead, share your own preferences as a way to start the conversation: "You might have noticed that I am more of a conflict seeker. I don't shy away from arguments, and I tend to get worked up quickly." You could also share tactful observations about what you've noticed about your counterpart. "Based on how you responded to Corinne's questioning in this morning's meeting, it seems as if you prefer to steer away from conflict. Is that right?"

You're trying to learn what someone's style is, not judge it. Instead of saying "We've got a problem here because it seems as if you don't know how to discuss conflict," you might ask, "What do you do in your culture when people disagree?" It's better to ask questions than make statements, and use phrases that ask for confirmation, such as "Correct me if I'm wrong . . ." or "Do I have this right?" Meyer points out that there's nothing wrong with showing curiosity. "People always like to be asked about themselves," she says.

Once you learn more about the culture, use that knowledge to help you understand your situation better. Why did he speak to me like that? What did he mean? "If you're dealing with someone from the Netherlands and he speaks to you in a really direct way," says Meyer, "you can interpret that behavior differently than if someone from China was short with you." Was the person really being rude? Was he intentionally being vague and trying to hide something? Or is there a cultural reason for him to speak or behave like that?

If you come up empty-handed

If your digging doesn't turn up adequate information, all is not lost. Although it helps, having this information is not a prerequisite to a productive conversation. Instead, prepare by playing out a few scenarios. What if she's a conflict seeker and gets mad at me? What if he yells? What if she's an avoider and gets upset? Or tries to leave the room?

You may even want to role-play with another co-worker. If you do, Jen Su suggests you play your counterpart and your coworker acts as you. That will help you take your counterpart's perspective and ask yourself, How would I want that person to interact with me? This will also allow you to better understand how your counterpart sees you.

How Your Styles Work Together

Now that you have a sense of your approach to conflict and have gleaned some insights into your counterpart's preferences, how will your styles interact? If you're both seekers, can you expect an all-out brawl? If you're both avoiders, should you forget the idea of directly addressing the conflict? See table 4-1 to get a sense of what typically happens between each of the types and how you might manage it.

Identify the Type of Conflict

Next, think about what's causing the conflict. Review the four types of conflict I identified in chapter 1, "Types

TABLE 4-1

How conflict approaches work together

	You are an *avoider*	You are a *seeker*
Your counterpart is an *avoider*	**What happens:** • Both of you lean toward doing nothing. • You may tamp down feelings that could explode later on. **How to manage:** • One of you needs to take the lead. • Say directly, "I know we both don't like conflict, but instead of doing nothing, should we consider other options?" • Do your best to draw the person out in a sensitive, thoughtful way. • If things get tough, don't shy away. Fight your natural instinct.	**What happens:** • You tend to bulldoze your counterpart into agreeing with you. • Your counterpart may act passive-aggressively to get his point across. **How to manage:** • Ask the person to participate actively in the conversation—not hide her opinions. • Don't be a bully. • Be patient with the pacing of the conversation.
Your counterpart is a *seeker*	**What happens:** • You are tempted to play the role of "good guy" and go along with what your counterpart wants. • You might get trampled by your counterpart's requests. **How to manage:** • Explicitly ask for what you need: "To have a productive conversation, I need you to be patient with me and watch the tone and volume of your voice." • Earn the seeker's respect by being direct and to the point. • Don't signal disrespect, which is likely to set the seeker off.	**What happens:** • Neither of you is afraid to say what's on your mind. • The discussion turns contentious. • You might end up saying things you don't believe. • You both feel disrespected. **How to manage:** • Since you'll both be eager to address the situation, take extra time to prepare for the conversation. • Know that you're likely to feel impatient and schedule your discussion in a way that allows you both to take breaks. • Be ready—things may get heated. Suggest a coffee break or a walk or a change of scenery to help even out emotions.

Source: Adapted from an interview with Amy Jen Su, coauthor with Muriel Maignan Wilkins of *Own the Room: Discover Your Signature Voice to Master Your Leadership Presence* (Boston: Harvard Business Review Press, 2013).

of Conflict," and suss out whether your disagreement is over issues related to relationship, task, process, or status (see table 1-1).

Go over what's happened so far with your counterpart—what she's said and done, who else has been involved, where the disagreement started, and what it's related to. With all that information, ask yourself: Are we disagreeing about the goal of a project, or how to achieve it? Does my counterpart think she should be leading the initiative? Have we exchanged barbs? Or all of the above?

Rarely do conflicts fall into just one of these categories, so try to identify each type of conflict that's occurring. Doing this helps you to:

- **Organize your own thoughts.** In the midst of a conflict, rational thinking often goes out the window. Considering what type of conflict you're having will help you set aside your emotional reactions and structure your thinking. If you decide to directly address the situation, parsing the conflict into categories will set you up for a successful conversation (see chapter 5, "Get Ready for the Conversation").

- **Identify common ground.** By labeling your differences of opinion, you'll also see where you and your counterpart concur. If you disagree on how exactly to compensate a customer who received bad service (process), you may note that you agree on the need to make the customer happy (task).

This shared goal becomes a foundation for reaching a resolution (see chapter 6, "Have a Productive Conversation").

- **Structure the conversation.** Before you begin your discussion with your counterpart, create a list of the types of conflict you're experiencing and the specific issues you disagree on. This will help guide your conversation and keep you focused on the issue at hand.

Be particularly careful when labeling a disagreement a "relationship conflict." Many disagreements do end up here, but personalities are not always to blame, says Ben Dattner, author of *The Blame Game: How the Hidden Rules of Credit and Blame Determine Our Success or Failure.* "More often than not, the real underlying cause of workplace strife is the situation itself rather than the people involved." What people *think* they're fighting about isn't actually what they *are* fighting about. For example, they might perceive the root cause of the struggle to be a personality clash when in fact it's a process conflict.

Dattner explains: "Perhaps the conflict is due to someone on the team simply not doing her job, in which case talking about personality as being the cause of conflict is a dangerous distraction from the real issue . . . Focusing too much on either hypothetical or irrelevant causes of conflict may work in the short term, but it creates the risk over the long term that the underlying causes will never be addressed or fixed."

Determine Your Goal

Before you decide which approach to take, determine what you hope to accomplish. Keeping in mind the personalities of the people involved, their communication styles, and the type of conflict you're having, reflect on your ultimate goal: Do you want to complete the project quickly? To deliver the best results you can? Does your relationship with this person matter more than the outcome of the work? Figure out what you need to get done. If you're under pressure to complete a presentation by a certain date and your counterpart in sales is complaining about how much data you need from him, you might consider doing nothing so that you can get the numbers you need and hit your deadline. Later you could explain to the sales guy how his griping impacted you and ask what would work better for him for future requests.

If you're having more than one type of conflict, you might set more than one goal. For example, if you're fighting with your conflict-seeking boss about which metrics to report to the senior leadership team (task conflict) and you and your boss have exchanged heated emails that challenge each other's understanding of web analytics (relationship conflict), your goal may be to come up with a set of stats that you can both live with *and* to make sure that your boss understands that you respect her and her expertise.

Make sure your goal is reasonable, suggests IMD's Jean-François Manzoni, who has conducted extensive research on conflict management. Ask yourself: Does what I want make sense? Is it realistic? If not, set your sights a little lower. Come up with a small, manageable goal, such as "agreeing on which of us will own the re-design project" or "creating a six-week plan for how our team will collaborate." If you're disagreeing over how to proceed on an important project, your goal might be to end the conversation by simply agreeing on the next step rather than cementing a full implementation plan.

It's not uncommon, particularly with relationship conflict, to want to set a goal that's about changing the other person. Perhaps you'd like to show your colleague that her passive-aggressive behavior doesn't work or make sure your boss knows what a jerk he's been for the past week. But these kinds of agendas are better dropped before they lead to full-on fights.

"It's easy to become aggravated by other people's actions and forget what you were trying to achieve in the first place," says Jeffrey Pfeffer, of Stanford's Graduate School of Business. But it's not likely you're going to change the other person, so focus on your goal. If the conflict were over and you found that you had won, what would that look like?

Pick Your Option

Now it's time to decide what to do. Taking into account your goal, and the other person's natural tendency and communication style, which of the four options discussed in chapter 2 is best for handling the specific situation you're in (see table 4-2)?

There is no magic formula that tells you which approach to take. It's not like two conflict seekers having a

TABLE 4-2

The four options for addressing conflict

The option	What it is	Use it when . . .
Do nothing	Ignoring and swallowing the conflict	• You don't have the energy or time. • You suspect the other person is unwilling to have a constructive conversation. • You have little or no power. • You won't beat yourself up or stew about it.
Address indirectly	Skirting the issue instead of naming it	• It's important in your culture to save face. • You work in a place where direct confrontation is inappropriate. • You think the other person will be more willing to take feedback from someone else.
Address directly	Actively trying to change the situation by talking to the other person	• You worry that there will be lingering resentment if you don't clear the air. • You've tried other options and the problem persists. • You want to get your relationship with your counterpart back on track.
Exit	Getting out of the situation entirely by being reassigned to another project, finding a new boss, or leaving the company	• You're dealing with someone from another department or outside your company where your jobs aren't interdependent. • You can easily find a job somewhere else. • You've tried other options and nothing has worked.

relationship conflict who want to restore a friendly rapport should always use the "address directly" approach. The reality is that the option you choose depends on all of the above factors as well as other circumstances, such as your office norms or the amount of time pressure you're under. Play out each option in your head and assess the pros and cons for your specific situation. If you do nothing, will you be able to let go of the conflict? If you directly confront, will your counterpart be able to engage constructively? There is no one right answer; there's just the one that's right for you and the circumstances you're in. (See also the sidebar "Know When to Walk Away.")

Be mindful of your natural tendency

Because the conflict may have triggered a fight-or-flight response in your brain, your immediate response—"We need to address this right away" or "I'm going to find a new job"—may not be the best one. Conflict avoiders often gravitate toward the first two options (doing nothing or addressing the conflict indirectly), while seekers prefer the latter two (addressing directly or exiting). Keep this in mind when you're choosing your option. Ask yourself whether you're doing what's best for the situation—and will most likely help you achieve your goal—or if you're opting for an approach that's most comfortable for you.

Cool down before deciding

Brett says that it's wise to take a breather before choosing an approach. "Weighing whether to bring up and try to resolve a conflict should be a rational decision. The first question to ask yourself: Am I too emotional right now?" she says. If so, take a step back from the conflict. Return to your desk and take a few deep breaths. Go for a walk outside. Or sleep on it. You want to be sure whatever route you choose is based on a lucid decision, not a rash one.

KNOW WHEN TO WALK AWAY

It's not an easy decision to walk away from a conflict—temporarily or permanently. But it's important to recognize when the situation calls for it. "If you're angry or upset—or your colleague is—it's not a good time to engage. It won't help if either of you is yelling or pounding the table," says Jeanne Brett. She explains that there's a lot of research that shows people are unable to be rational when their emotions are high (see more on managing your emotions in chapter 6).

Judith White, a leadership professor at the Tuck School of Business at Dartmouth, says there are several signs that you need to walk away—at least temporarily:

- Your counterpart is yelling or is otherwise out of control.

- You feel as if you're going to lose control in any way that might be dangerous to you, your counterpart, or your relationship.

- The fight is happening in a public setting where others can see or hear you.

- It becomes obvious that the discussion can't be resolved through the current conversation. You or your counterpart repeating the same argument over and over is the telltale sign here.

- Your colleague has never demonstrated a willingness to concede.

(continued)

KNOW WHEN TO WALK AWAY

(*continued*)

- The damage is already done. For example, maybe the project you're fighting over ended last week and the decision can't be reversed.

Once you've made the tough decision to walk away, how do you actually do it? Here are some tips:

- If the situation feels overly heated or dangerous, simply walk away. Leave the room, go to the bathroom, or take a walk outside the building.

- If you can, explain that you need some time to think through the conflict before coming back to it. "Don't ever tell someone he or she needs to calm down, because the person will lose face or only become more upset," advises White. (For more sample language examples, see chapter 2, "Your Options for Handling Conflict.")

- Take the time you need to cool down (or let your counterpart cool down). When you feel ready to make a smart and thoughtful choice about how to address the conflict, you can return to it.

Here's an example. Jonathan was meeting with his project manager, Rebecca, about why they were falling behind in their deadlines. As a conflict seeker, he was asking pointed questions to get at the root of what was behind the delays. Rebecca was getting more and more agitated as Jonathan went line by line through the plan. Soon Rebecca snapped. She stood up and pointed her finger at Jonathan, accusing him of badgering her. "This is your fault, not mine," she said. Jonathan quickly apologized for pushing so hard, but Rebecca wouldn't hear it. She yelled, "I don't need your apologies. I need you to stop %^@# harassing me." Jonathan realized he was stuck. Rebecca had lost control, and he didn't feel like anything he said would help. He stood up and said, "I'm sorry that this conversation has taken this turn. I'm going to go back to my desk to think through how we might resolve this. It'd be great if we could regroup tomorrow." Rebecca sent him an apology later that night, and when they had both calmed down the next day, they were able to have a more rational conversation about how to get the project back on track.

Sometimes delaying a tense conversation by a day helps, as it did with Rebecca and Jonathan. But sometimes, a day is not enough. You may be faced with a situation in which you decide to permanently walk away—by either doing nothing or exiting the relationship entirely. Whether or not you do this, says White, depends on two questions: How important is this relationship? How potentially valuable is this deal? As

(continued)

KNOW WHEN TO WALK AWAY

(*continued*)

Deepak Malhotra and Max H. Bazerman point out in *Negotiation Genius: How to Overcome Obstacles and Achieve Brilliant Results at the Bargaining Table and Beyond,* you shouldn't negotiate when the costs of negotiation exceed the potential gains.

Exiting the relationship is particularly advisable when the situation is causing you extreme discomfort—your health is suffering, for example. If you can't concentrate on anything else or are having panic attacks, there's no sense enduring more torture. Also, if your counterpart is singling you out and trying to prevent you from doing your job, it's time to take extreme measures. Speak to someone else, such as your boss or an HR representative, to see what support is available to you.

In a highly emotional conflict—in which one or both parties are extremely angry or upset—it can be tempting to exercise the exit option. But even situations in which feelings are running high can benefit from you opting to address it, or even doing nothing. Judith White says: "It's natural for people to feel strong emotion in a conflict situation. Once the conflict is identified and addressed, and parties are allowed to vent, emotion usually dissipates . . . Recognize the emotion, but don't let it stop you from negotiating."

Adapt Your Approach

Managing conflict is a fluid process. You may start with one approach and then find you need to switch to another if your selected approach is no longer working or the conflict grows or changes. For example, you may decide to directly address the situation by talking with your colleague about why you're disagreeing over the targets each of your teams should be hitting, but then find that you're getting nowhere: Your coworker is unresponsive or, worse, frustrated that you don't agree with her and just gets angrier. Then you may decide to do nothing and move on. You could also start with the do-nothing option and realize that the problem is getting worse, so you need to address it directly, by talking with your colleague, or indirectly, by going to your boss. As you weigh the options for your specific situation, you don't have to make a choice and stick to it no matter what. You can always change tactics as your conflict plays out.

Consider this example. Amara and Vivek work closely in a small design group. Amara has to complete her initial designs before Vivek can take over the presentations and do the formatting that is his responsibility. In a team meeting, Vivek made an offhand comment about Amara "taking her time" with the latest batch of presentations. Amara thought about the statement, and even talked about it with another colleague, and she concluded that it could be interpreted in several ways, but the implication was that Amara's speed was impacting Vivek's work. Amara tends to avoid conflict, so she didn't like the idea of bringing it up with Vivek. Plus they had worked well together for so long. She didn't see the point.

She thought she could let it go. And for a few weeks, she did. But soon she realized that it was still bothering her. Every time she handed something off to Vivek, she mentally replayed his saying "She's taking her time," so she decided to address the situation directly. She scheduled an appointment with Vivek to ask what he had meant and to find a way to move forward.

The fluidity of the process can work the other way, too. Take Marie's story. She called one of her long-time vendors to directly address and explain that her company's payment terms had changed. In the middle of the conversation, Claude, the finance manager at the vendor, hung up on her. She emailed him and said that she'd like to set up a time to talk. But when they got on the phone again, Claude wouldn't say anything other than "This doesn't work for us." Marie was offended and frustrated. Recognizing that the direct approach wasn't working, she decided to go to Claude's boss and appeal to him. She didn't want to get Claude in trouble, but they clearly weren't able to resolve the conflict on their own. Soon after she spoke with Claude's manager and explained the situation, Claude called her and offered to negotiate the terms.

The next two chapters talk about preparing for and conducting a conversation if you've decided to address the conflict directly. Even if you've chosen one of the other options, your approach may change, so it's best to be prepared.

CHAPTER 5

Get Ready for the Conversation

Once you've resolved to directly address the conflict, it's tempting to have the conversation immediately. But taking time to prepare will help you remain calm and increase the chances that you and your counterpart will come away with a better solution than either of you could have predicted.

Below are several guidelines to help you prepare for a productive discussion.

Check Your Mindset

If you're getting yourself ready for a conversation that you've labeled "difficult," you're more likely to feel nervous, stressed, angry, or upset. To minimize those negative emotions, try to think about it as a non-charged conversation, suggests Jean-François Manzoni. For example, instead of giving negative feedback, you're having a constructive conversation about development. Or you're not saying "no" to your boss; you're offering up an alternative solution.

"A difficult conversation tends to go best when you think about it as just a normal conversation," says Holly Weeks, a communications expert. This isn't sugarcoating. Be honest with yourself about how hard the conversation might be, but also put as constructive a frame on it as possible. You might tell yourself: We may have to talk about difficult things, but we'll work through them together because Carol and I have always respected each other.

And focus on what you stand to gain from the conversation. "Assume you have something to learn; assume there is a more creative solution than you've thought of," says Jeff Weiss, author of the *HBR Guide to Negotiating*. By entering the discussion with an open mind, regardless of your coworker's stance, you're more likely to find common ground.

Take Your Counterpart's Perspective

Try to get a sense of what your colleague might be thinking. Ideally you already did some thinking about this when you analyzed the conflict, but go a little deeper. She had a rationale for the way she's behaved so far (even if you don't agree with it). What might that reason be? "Try to imagine your way into their shoes as best you can. You can learn a lot by doing that simple mental exercise," says Jonathan Hughes. Think about what's going on for them. Ask yourself: What would I do if I were her, or if I were in R&D instead of marketing? What if I were someone reporting to me? What if I were my boss? Also ask yourself: What is she trying to achieve in the conflict? You'll need a sense of what her goal is if you want to resolve it. Identify places where you see eye to eye on the issues. This common ground will give you a foundation to joint problem-solve.

Ask a colleague what he thinks is going on in your counterpart's mind. Make sure it's someone you trust, says Hughes. You might say something like, "I'd love some advice and coaching. I haven't worked much with Akiko before, but I know you have. Can you help me understand how she might be seeing this situation?" Don't use the conversation to vent and seek validation. "Paint the situation for him as neutrally as you can," says Karen Dillon, author of the *HBR Guide to Office Politics*. "Cataloging every fault and misstep will probably get you sympathy but not constructive feedback, so focus on the problem."

It's unlikely that you'll be able to gather all the information you want about your colleague and her interests before you sit down together. Weiss says, "Craft a set of questions to ask in the room to uncover critical information and test any hypotheses you made." This will help you, once you're face-to-face, to show that you care enough about her perspective to think it through beforehand and to discover more about how she views the situation.

In addition to thinking about your counterpart's take on the situation, remember the work you did in the previous chapter to consider his natural tendency for handling conflict and his communication style.

Consider the Larger Organizational Context

While the conflict may revolve around you and your counterpart, the reality is that you're both part of a broader context—that of your organization or your industry. Consider how the larger playing field you're operating in might be affecting the conflict.

First, determine the culture of your organization or team. Do people in your unit generally try to avoid conflict? Or is it acceptable to have heated debates? Are you at odds with an external vendor and feeling less invested in working things out because you have several other partners who are courting your business? How might the larger culture be shaping the current conflict you're having? Is it making it worse than it needs to be?

Hughes points out that quite a few years ago Microsoft had a reputation for having an aggressive culture. "During your first few presentations their people would just tear into you. The culture was one that valued conflict. 'We're going to use rigorous, fiery debate to separate good from bad ideas,'" he says. In a company like this, which places a premium on being direct, you'd need to be prepared for a lively debate and know not to take criticism personally. On the other hand, there are companies where consensus is the norm. "In these places, you're going to take a slower, more iterative approach to conflict," says Hughes.

Second, reflect on the current circumstances surrounding your organization. Are there potential layoffs looming? Have budgets been cut? Is your industry on a downward trend? Your conflict may be intensified when tensions are high in the company, or it might take on a more severe or vicious tone. The answers to these questions may not change the approach you choose, but you should consider them as you get ready for the discussion. Also find out who else in the organization can help you both reach a resolution. Are there colleagues who need to be involved in the discussions? Should you consult your boss or HR?

Plan Your Message

Think about what you'll say when you get in the room *before* you get in the room, incorporating your goal and your colleague's perspective, interests, and style. What do you want your counterpart to take away from the conversation? "You'll have a better chance of being heard if you define your message and decide how you'll convey it," says Dillon. Plan how you'll approach the conversation—literally what you will and won't say. "View it as a presentation," suggests Dillon. "What information does your counterpart need to hear? Identify the key points you'd like to make, highlighting mutual benefits when possible." When you frame the conversation as trying to achieve a shared goal—such as meeting a deadline, coming in under budget, or having a positive work relationship—the conversation will go better.

But don't script the entire conversation. That's a waste of time. "It's very unlikely that it will go according to your plan," says Weeks. Your counterpart doesn't know "his lines," so when he "goes off script, you have no forward motion" and the exchange "becomes weirdly artificial." Your strategy for the conversation should be "flexible" and contain "a repertoire of possible responses," says Weeks. Jot down notes and key points before your conversation. Even with thoughtful planning, it's not uncommon for there to be misalignment between what you mean when you say something (your intention) and what the other person hears (your impact). "It doesn't matter if your intent is honorable if your impact is not," says Linda Hill, a leadership professor at Harvard Business School. Most people are very aware of what they meant to say but are less tuned in to what the other person heard or how they interpreted it. So choose your words wisely, and try to anticipate and address anything that might be misinterpreted (see chapter 6, "Have a Productive Conversation," for more discussion tips).

Prepare for Multiple Scenarios

Since you can't know how the conversation is going to go, you may want to play out a few scenarios, suggests Amy Jen Su. Find a trusted colleague with whom you can do a few role-plays. What if your counterpart gets upset and cries? What if she gets angry? Try responding using different approaches and test out phrases you might use for various possibilities. And ask your role-play partner to give you feedback.

Pick the Right Time

Knowing exactly when to have the conversation can be challenging. On the one hand, it might be easiest to get it over with quickly, when all the details are fresh in your mind. On the other hand, as discussed in the previous chapter, it's often a good idea for everyone to cool down before trying to get into problem-solving mode. Here are some tips on picking the right time:

- **Consider your tendency.** Check yourself before you decide to delay or get into the conversation. If you're a seeker, you're likely to want to get going and have the conversation. But if your counterpart is an avoider, he may need more time. And if you're an avoider, you may want to put the conversation off, but watch that you're not using that tactic as an "out" so that you don't have to face the issue at all.

- **Take into account any outside deadlines.** Sometimes you don't have the luxury of several days or weeks to work out your disagreement. If the budget you're fighting over is due to the executive committee by the end of the month and it's the 28th, you need to have the conversation sooner rather than later.

- **Check the emotions.** As discussed in the previous chapter, it's better to have the conversation when you and your counterpart can be level-headed. Ask yourself: Am I too emotional right now? If so, you may say the wrong thing, embarrass yourself or your colleague, or create awkward scenes for others. In those instances, take a walk around the building, or change your surroundings by working in a small conference room or heading home to work in peace.

"Occasionally, you need to let it go and come back to it another time when you can both have the conversation," says Hill. It's OK to walk away and return to the discussion later. But if you decide to put off the conversation, make a plan for when you will have it so that you don't keep delaying it.

When you're ready, set up a meeting. Look for a time when you'll both be in a good frame of mind. "Not first thing on Monday when you're both coming in to a full inbox. Not last thing on Friday when you're eager for the weekend to begin," says Dillon. Be sure to schedule enough time so that you'll be able to reach a conclusion, or at least end in a constructive place where you can agree to meet again. In fact, you may want to have an initial meeting to hear each other out and then schedule a follow-up time when you can dig in to how to solve the disagreement after you've both had time to reflect on what the other person said.

Choose the Right Place

The venue will have an effect on whether you both feel able to speak freely, express any emotions, and ultimately reach a resolution, so select a location where you'll both be comfortable. "Right after lunch in a neutral conference room? Over coffee at the local greasy spoon?" suggests Dillon. You might take a walk outside together for a change of scenery. Avoid choosing a place that gives you or your counterpart an advantage. Inviting someone into your office puts you in a power position, for example, because it's your space and you're the one sitting behind a desk. And when choosing a conference room, think about who's in adjacent rooms. Sometimes walls are thinner than you think.

Ideally you want the conversation to happen face-to-face in private. "Don't try to solve differences using email, which does not do a good job of conveying tone or nuance," says Dillon. If the issue starts on email, send a gentle request such as "Could we continue this discussion in person?" or just call the person.

If you have a conflict with one person during a meeting, don't attempt to work it out in front of the group, even if others in the room have a stake in the outcome. It's better to take the conversation off-line and then report back to the group. For example, if you and a colleague start to debate the specific marketing language that will accompany the rollout of a new product and the conversation gets heated, you might say, "Tom and I seem to have the strongest viewpoints on this. Would it be OK with you, Tom, if we paused here and continued the discussion after the meeting? Then we can come back to the group with our recommendation." This will give you and Tom time to cool down, make sure you don't embarrass yourselves in front of everyone, and allow you to have a more candid and fruitful discussion later.

Vent

Before you get into the room, find a trusted colleague or a spouse or friend who can listen to you complain. Say everything you feel about the situation—the good, the bad, and the ugly. Don't hold back. Susan David, a psychologist and coauthor of the *Harvard Business Review* article "Emotional Agility," says that "suppressing your emotions—deciding not to say something when you're upset—can lead to bad results." She explains that if you don't express your emotions, they're likely to show up elsewhere.

Psychologists call this *emotional leakage*. "Have you ever yelled at your spouse or child after a frustrating day at work—a frustration that had nothing to do with him or her? When you bottle up your feelings, you're likely to express your emotions in unintended ways instead, either sarcastically or in a completely different context. Suppressing your emotions is associated with poor memory, difficulties in relationships, and physiological costs (such as cardiovascular health problems)," David explains. Prevent your emotions from seeping out—in the conversation or at home—by getting your feelings out ahead of time. You'll be more centered and calm when you're having the discussion.

Table 5-1 summarizes the guidelines. Use this checklist to prepare mentally, strategically, and logistically for your discussion.

When You Have No Time to Prepare

Sometimes there's no time to do this advance work. A decision needs to be made immediately, or your colleague catches you off guard, or your boss storms into

TABLE 5-1

Your pre-conversation checklist

MENTALLY

	Do	Don't
☐ CHECK YOUR MINDSET Be positive, but also honest with yourself about how difficult the conversation may be. ☐ CONSIDER THE OTHER POSITIONS Look at the situation from your counterpart's perspective: What does she want? ☐ VENT Get your emotions out beforehand so you can be calm during the conversation.	• Focus on what you stand to gain from the discussion and assume you have something to learn. • Ask a trusted co-worker for input if you're at a loss about what your counterpart is thinking. • Identify places where you see eye to eye. • Get your feelings out ahead of time so you'll be more centered and calm. • Come up with a list of questions you want to ask when you sit down together.	• Label the conversation as "difficult." • Sugarcoat what's going to happen. • Assume you can know everything your counterpart is thinking ahead of time. • Vent to a friend who typically riles you up.

STRATEGICALLY

	Do	Don't
☐ PLAN YOUR MESSAGE Think about what you'll say ahead of time. ☐ PREPARE FOR MULTIPLE SCENARIOS Play out various ways the conversation might go.	• Plan how you'll approach the conversation—literally what you will and won't say. • Focus on a shared goal. • Find a trusted colleague with whom you can do a few role-plays. • Test out phrases you might say.	• Script the entire conversation—just jot down notes and key points. • Assume you know how the conversation is going to go.

(continued)

71

TABLE 5-1 *(continued)*

LOGISTICALLY		
	Do	**Don't**
☐ PICK THE RIGHT TIME Choose a time when you and your counterpart can be unrushed and calm. ☐ SELECT THE RIGHT PLACE Look for somewhere you can meet in private.	• Pick a time when you and your counterpart won't be rushed. • Consider an initial meeting to hear each other out, and then schedule a follow-up time when you can focus on problem-solving. • Talk in person, or at least on the phone. • Try a change of scenery—going to a coffee shop or taking a walk.	• Have the conversation over email • Try to talk to your colleague when emotions are high. • Have a fight in a group setting (such as in a team meeting). • Choose a "turf" setting where you or your counterpart has a power advantage.

your office. Jeanne Brett suggests you try to put off the conversation if at all feasible. You might say, "I see that this is a problem, and I'd like to take some time to think about ways to resolve it. I promise I'll come by your office tomorrow to discuss it." It's important to not be dismissive and to acknowledge your colleague's feelings—"I can see you're really upset about this"—and then ask whether you can set a time to talk when you're both calmer. If your counterpart insists that you have the discussion right then, you might have to go ahead. "The best you can do in these situations is to remain calm and stop yourself from getting into a negative emotional spiral," says Brett. (See chapter 6 for more on how to maintain your composure and manage your emotions.)

You may be wondering, Do I really need to do all of this for one 10-minute conversation? The answer is yes. While it takes time (though it will get easier the more you do it), there is a huge payoff. You'll go into the conversation with the right mindset, feeling confident, knowing what you want to achieve. This foundation is the key to a productive discussion.

CHAPTER 6

Have a Productive Conversation

You're now ready to have a constructive discussion. Your goal is to work with your counterpart to better understand "the underlying causes of the problem and what you can do to solve it together," says Jeanne Brett.

First, frame the discussion so that you and your counterpart start off on the right foot. Then there are three things you'll do simultaneously as the conversation flows: Manage your emotions, listen well, and be heard.

When you sit down with your counterpart, don't be overly wedded to the information you've gathered in advance. Be flexible. "You don't want to be so prepared that you anticipate a particular reaction and you're not able to take in what's actually happening," says Amy Jen Su. If you see the behavior you expected, then label it (in your head) and continue to observe. But allow yourself to be surprised, too. The same goes for cultural norms.

"Knowing something about your colleague's culture gives you hypotheses to test. But just because you have an East Asian at the table doesn't mean he will be indirect," says Brett.

Frame the Conversation

Your first few sentences can make or break the rest of the discussion. Set the conversation up for success by establishing common ground between you and your counterpart, labeling the type of conflict you're having, asking your counterpart for advice, laying out ground rules, and focusing on the future. Here's more on how to do that.

Focus on common ground

"Too often we end up framing a conflict as who's right or who's wrong," Linda Hill says. Instead of trying to understand what's really happening in a disagreement, we advocate for our position. Hill admits that it's normal to be defensive and even to blame the other person, but implying "You're wrong" will make matters worse. Instead, state what you agree on. In chapter 4, when you identified the type of conflict you're having, you noted where there was common ground, and in chapter 5, you identified where your goals might overlap. Put those commonalities out there as a way to connect. "We both want to make sure our patients get the best care possible" or "We agree that the new email system should integrate with our existing IT systems" or "We both want our department to get adequate funding."

If you weren't able to pinpoint something that you both agreed on beforehand or you're not sure you know what your counterpart's goal is, the easiest way to find out is to ask, says Jonathan Hughes, "although sometimes people need help crystallizing their goals." Explain what's important to you and then ask, "Is there any overlap with what you care about? Or do you have another goal?" Asking questions like these sets a collaborative tone.

Label the type of conflict

Acknowledge the type of conflict you're having—relationship, task, process, or status—and check with your counterpart that he sees it the same way. "It seems as if the crux of our disagreement is about where to launch the product first. Do you agree?" You may also want to reassure him that you value your relationship. This will convey to him that your point of contention is not a personal one. Say something like, "I really respect you and how you run your department. This is not about our relationship, but about how our two teams will work together on this project."

If your conflict covers several different types, as many do, name each one in turn so that they're all out on the table. Hughes suggests you say something along these lines: *It feels like we agree on the same goal here—to bring in revenue from this new product as soon as possible.* [Establishing common ground on task] *Our conflict seems to be more about how we do it—the timing of how quickly we roll out this product and whether we roll it out in target markets first.* [Labeling the process conflict] *In addition to that disagreement over the means, it seems—and I could be wrong about this—you feel some*

frustration with me about how I've approached this.
[Naming the relationship conflict] *I want to put that all on the table because success is going to depend on us working together.*

Ask for advice

Research by Katie Liljenquist at Brigham Young University's Department of Organizational Leadership and Strategy and Adam Galinsky, the chair of the Management Department at the Columbia Business School, has shown that asking for advice makes you appear more warm, humble, and cooperative—all of which can go a long way in resolving a conflict. "Being asked for advice is inherently flattering because it's an implicit endorsement of our opinions, values, and expertise. Furthermore, it works equally well up and down the hierarchy—subordinates are delighted and empowered by requests for their insights, and superiors appreciate the deference to their authority and experience," say Liljenquist and Galinsky. Of course, any goodwill garnered by this tactic will swiftly be undone if you ignore your counterpart's suggestions. Incorporate at least some small part of what she advises into your approach.

There are two other benefits to framing a conflict as a request for advice, according to Liljenquist and Galinsky. First, you nudge your counterpart to see things from your perspective. "The last time someone came to you for advice, most likely, you engaged in an instinctive mental exercise: You tried to put yourself in the other person's shoes and imagine the world through his eyes," they explain. The second benefit is that an adversary-turned-advisor may well become a champion for your cause. "When someone offers you advice, it represents an investment of his time and energy. Your request empowers your advisor to make good on his recommendations and become an advocate," they say.

Set up ground rules

The conversation will go more smoothly if you agree on a code of conduct. At a minimum, suggest no interrupting, no yelling, and no personal attacks. This is especially important for conflict seekers, who may see no problem in raising their voices. Acknowledge that you both may need to take a break at some point. Then ask what other rules are important to your counterpart. If you're concerned your colleague won't abide by the rules, write them down on a piece of paper to keep in front of you or on a whiteboard if you're in a conference room. If your counterpart begins to raise his voice, for example, you can nod toward the written rules and offer a gentle reminder. "We said we weren't going to yell. Can you lower your voice?" These rules may also be helpful if you need to change the tone of the conversation later on (see "Change the tenor of the conversation" later in the chapter).

Focus on the future

It's tempting to rehash everything that's happened up to this point. But it's generally not helpful to go over every detail or to focus too heavily on the past. "You can't resolve a battle over a problem that has already happened, but you can set a course going forward," says Judith White. Focus the discussion on solving the problem and moving on. You can start by saying "I know a lot has gone on between us. If it's OK with you, I'd like to talk about what we both might do to make sure this project gets completed on budget and how we can better work together in the future." If your counterpart starts to harp on the past, don't chastise her for it. Instead, refocus the conversation by saying something like "I hear you. How can we make sure that doesn't happen again?"

Each of these steps will establish the right tone for your conversation: that you and your counterpart are in it together and you need to reach a resolution that works for both of you.

Manage Your Emotions—and Theirs

Conflict can bring up all sorts of negative emotions for seekers and avoiders alike. Recognize the emotion, but don't let it stop you from having the conversation. To watch your own reaction while also recognizing your counterpart's feelings, understand why conflict can feel so bad. Remain calm, acknowledge and label your feelings, and allow for venting. Let's take a closer look at how to manage emotions and clear the way for a productive discussion.

Understand why you're so uncomfortable

In the middle of a tough conversation, it can be difficult to take a deep breath and think rationally about what to do next. This is because you're fighting your body's natural reaction, says psychiatry professor John Ratey. Your brain experiences conflict, particularly relationship conflict, as a threat: *I disagree with you. You haven't done your job. I don't like what you just said. You're wrong. I hate you.*

Leadership expert Annie McKee suggests that conflict makes us feel bad because it means we're going to have to give something up—our point of view, the way we're used to doing something, or maybe even power. That threat triggers your sympathetic nervous system. As a result, your heart rate and breathing rate spike, your muscles tighten, the blood in your body moves away from your organs. "Some people feel their stomach tense as acid moves into it," says Ratey.

Depending on the perceived size and intensity of the threat, you may then move into fight-or-flight mode. "When you're panicking, feeling crushed or over-whelmed, the body's response is to be aggressive—punch or push back—or to run away and hide," says Ratey. "This is when you're in it full-time and the discomfort goes all over your body. It's like seeing a bunch of snakes or spiders in front of you." When your brain perceives danger like this, it can be difficult to make rational decisions, which is precisely what you need to do in a difficult conversation. Luckily, it's possible to interrupt this physical response and restore calm in your body.

Remain calm

There are several things you can do to keep your cool during a conversation or to calm yourself down if you've gotten worked up. For conflict seekers, it's especially important to keep your temper in check. For avoiders, these tactics will help keep you from retreating from the conversation.

- **Take a deep breath.** Notice the sensation of air coming in and out of your lungs. Feel it pass through your nostrils or down the back of your throat. This will take your attention off the physical signs of panic and keep you centered.

- **Focus on your body.** "Standing up and walking around may activate the thinking part of your brain," says Ratey, and keep you from exploding. If you and your counterpart are seated at a table, instead of leaping to your feet, you can say, "I feel like I need to stretch some. Mind if I walk around a bit?" If that doesn't feel comfortable, do small things like crossing two fingers or placing your feet firmly on the ground and noticing what the floor feels like on the bottom of your shoes.

- **Look around the room.** Become more aware of the space between you and your counterpart, suggests Jen Su. Notice the color of the walls or any artwork hanging there. Watch the hands of the clock move. "Pay attention to the whole room," she says. "This will help you realize that there's more space in the room than you're currently allowing."

- **Say a mantra.** Jen Su also recommends repeating a phrase to yourself to remind you to stay calm. Some of her clients have found "Go to neutral" to be a helpful prompt. You can also try "This isn't about me," "This will pass," or "This is about the business."

- **Take a break.** You may need to excuse yourself for a moment—get a cup of coffee or a glass of water, go to the bathroom, or take a brief stroll around the office. If you agreed up front that this might happen, you can say, "I think I need that break now. OK if we come back in five minutes?" If pushing pause wasn't on your list of ground rules, you can still make the request: "I'm sorry to interrupt you, but I'd love to get a cup of coffee before we continue. Can I get you something while I'm up?"

Acknowledge and label your feelings

When you're feeling emotional, "the attention you give your thoughts and feelings crowds your mind; there's no room to examine them," says Susan David. To get distance from the feeling, label it. "Just as you call a spade a spade, call a thought a thought and an emotion an emotion," says David. *He is so wrong about that and it's making me mad* becomes *I'm having the thought that my coworker is wrong, and I'm feeling anger.* Labeling like this allows you to see your thoughts and feelings for what they are: "transient sources of data that may or may not prove helpful." When you put that space between these emotions and you, it's easier to let them go—and not bury them or let them explode.

Allow for venting

You're probably not the only one who's upset. When your counterpart expresses anger or frustration, don't stop him. Let him vent as much as possible and remain calm while this is happening. Seekers may naturally do this, while you may have to draw an avoider out. If you took the time to air your own feelings with someone else (as discussed at the end of the previous chapter), you'll understand the importance of giving your counterpart this space. That's not to say it's easy. Brett explains:

> *It's hard not to yell back when you're being attacked, but that's not going to help. To remain calm while your colleague is venting and perhaps even hurling a few insults, visualize your coworker's words going over your shoulder, not hitting you in the chest. Don't act aloof; it's important to indicate that you're listening. But if you don't feed your counterpart's negative emotion with your own, it's likely he or she will wind down. Without the fuel of your equally strong reaction, he or she will run out of steam.*

Don't interrupt the venting or interject your own commentary. "Hold back and let your counterpart say his or her piece. You don't have to agree with it, but listen," Hill says. While you're doing this, you might be completely quiet or you might indicate you're listening by using phrases such as "I get that" or "I understand." Avoid saying anything that assigns feeling or blame, such as "Calm down" or "What you need to understand is . . ." This can be an explosive trigger for a conflict seeker. If you can tolerate the venting, without judging, you'll soon be able to guide the conversation to a more productive place. Refocus the conversation on the substance of the conflict by saying "I'm glad I got to hear how this has affected you. What do you think we should do next?" This will begin to draw out potential solutions so that you can move toward a resolution.

Listen Well

"If you listen to what the other person is saying, you're more likely to address the right issues and the conversation always ends up being better," says Jean-François Manzoni. Hear your counterpart out and ask questions. Here are tips for doing that.

Hear your coworker out

Even if you think you already understand your coworker's point of view—and you've put yourself in her shoes ahead of time—hear what she has to say. This is especially important if you aren't sure of what the other person sees as the root of the conflict. Acknowledge that you don't know, and ask. This shows your counterpart "that you care," Manzoni says. "Express your interest in understanding how the other person feels" and "take time to process the other person's words and tone," he adds. Be considerate and show compassion by validating what she's saying with phrases such as "I get it" or "I hear you." According to Jeff Weiss, this requires that you "stop figuring out your next line" and actively listen. Your coworker's explanation of his side may uncover an important piece of information that leads to a resolution. For example, if he says he's just trying to keep his boss happy, you can help him craft a resolution that addresses his boss's concerns.

Ask thoughtful questions

It's better to ask questions than to make statements; questions demonstrate your receptiveness to a genuine dialogue. This is when you bring in the questions you crafted in the previous chapter to unearth your counterpart's viewpoint and test your hypotheses (see the sidebar "Questions to Draw Out Your Counterpart's Perspective"). Once you've had a chance to hear her thoughts, Hill suggests you paraphrase and ask, "I think you said X. Did I get that right?"

Don't just take what she says at face value. This is especially important for a conflict avoider, who may not tell you all that she's thinking. Ask what her viewpoint looks like in action. For example, says team expert Liane Davey, "If you are concerned about a proposed course of action, ask your teammates to think through the impact of implementing their plan. 'OK, we're contemplating launching this product only to our U.S. customers. How is that going to land with our two big customers in Latin America?' This is less aggressive than saying 'Our Latin American customers will be angry.'" She adds: "Anytime you can demonstrate that you're open to ideas and curious about the right approach, it will open up the discussion."

Hill suggests you also get to the underlying reason for the initiative, policy, or approach that you're disagreeing with. You've already labeled the conflict as relationship, task, process, and/or status, but return to those categories in your questions to give your counterpart the opportunity to share her view. How do you see the goal

QUESTIONS TO DRAW OUT YOUR COUNTERPART'S PERSPECTIVE

- What about this situation is most troubling to you?

- What's most important to you?

- Can you tell me about the assumptions you've made here?

- Can you help me understand your thinking here?

- What makes you say that?

- Can you tell me more about that?

- What leads you to believe that?

- How does this relate to your other concerns?

- What would it take for us to be able to move forward? How do we get there?

- What would you like to see happen?

- What does a resolution look like for you?

- What ideas do you have that would meet both our needs?

- If this was completely in your control, how would you handle it?

differently? Why do you think you're the best person to lead the team?

Figure out why your counterpart thinks his idea is a reasonable proposal. Say something like, "Sam, I want to understand what we're trying to accomplish with this initiative. Can you go back and explain the reasoning behind it?" Get Sam to talk more about what he wants to achieve and why. It's not enough to know that he wants the project to be done in six months. You need to know why that's important to him. Is it because he made a promise to his boss? Is it because the team that's dedicated to the project needs to be freed up to take on an important client initiative? These are his underlying interests, and they'll help you later when you're trying to craft a resolution that incorporates his viewpoint (see chapter 7, "Get to a Resolution and Make a Plan").

You can return to the notion of asking for advice here. Perhaps you genuinely don't understand something, or you're shocked by something your counterpart has said. Davey suggests that you be mildly self-deprecating and own the misunderstanding. "If something is really surprising to you (you can't believe anyone would propose anything so crazy), say so. 'I think I'm missing something here. Tell me how this will address our sales gap for Q1.' This will encourage the person to restate his perspective and give you time to understand it."

Respectfully listening to and acknowledging your counterpart's viewpoint sets the stage for you to share your side of the conflict. If he feels heard, he's more likely to hear you out as well.

Be Heard

When it's time to share your story, allow your counterpart to understand your perspective in a genuine way. "Letting down your guard and letting the other person in may help her understand your point of view," says Mark Gerzon, author of *Leading Through Conflict: How Successful Leaders Transform Differences into Opportunities*. Help your coworker see where you're coming from by speaking from your own perspective, thinking before you talk, and watching body language (yours and hers) for clues that the conversation may be going off the rails.

Own your perspective

If you feel mistreated, you may be tempted to launch into your account of the events: "I want to talk about how horribly you treated me in that meeting." But that's unlikely to go over well.

Instead, treat your opinion like what it is: your opinion. Start sentences with "I," not "you." Say "I'm annoyed that this project is six months behind schedule," rather than "You've missed every deadline we've set." This will help the other person see your perspective and understand that you're not trying to blame him.

With a relationship conflict, explain exactly what is bothering you and follow up by identifying what you hope will happen. You might say, "I appreciate your ideas, but I'm finding it hard to hear them because throughout this process, I've felt as if you didn't respect my ideas. That's my perception. I'm not saying that it's your intention. I'd like to clear the air so that we can continue to work together to make the project a success."

Dorie Clark, author of *Reinventing You: Define Your Brand, Imagine Your Future,* says that you should admit blame when appropriate. "It's easy to demonize your colleague. But you're almost certainly contributing to the dynamic in some way, as well," Clark says. To get anywhere, you have to understand—and acknowledge—your role in the situation. Admitting your faults will help set a tone of accountability for both of you, and your counterpart is more likely to own up to her missteps as well. If she doesn't, and instead seizes on your confession and harps on it—"That's exactly why we're in this mess"—let it go. See it as part of the venting process described earlier.

Pay attention to your words

Sometimes, regardless of your good intentions, what you say can further upset your counterpart and make the issue worse. Other times you might say the exact thing that helps the person go from boiling mad to cool as a cucumber. See the sidebar "Phrases to Make Sure You've Heard." There are some basic rules you can follow to keep from pushing your counterpart's buttons. Of course you should avoid name-calling and finger-pointing. Focus on your perspective, as discussed above, avoiding sentences that start with "you" and could be misinterpreted as accusations. Your language should be "simple, clear, direct, and neutral," says Holly Weeks. Don't apologize for your feelings, either. The worst thing you can do "is to ask your counterpart to have sympathy for you,"

PHRASES TO MAKE SURE YOU'RE HEARD

- "Here's what I'm thinking."

- "My perspective is based on the following assumptions . . ."

- "I came to this conclusion because . . ."

- "I'd love to hear your reaction to what I just said."

- "Do you see any flaws in my reasoning?"

- "Do you see the situation differently?"

she says. Don't say things like "I feel so bad about saying this" or "This is really hard for me to do," because it takes the focus away from the problem and toward your own neediness. While this can be hard, especially for conflict avoiders, this language can make your counterpart feel obligated to focus on making you feel better before moving on.

Davey provides two additional rules when it comes to what you say:

- **Say "and," not "but."** "When you need to disagree with someone, express your contrary opinion as an 'and.' It's not necessary for someone else to be wrong for you to be right," she says. When you're surprised to hear something your counterpart has said, don't interject with a "But that's not right!" Just add your perspective. Davey suggests something like this: "You think we need to leave room in the budget for a customer event, and I'm concerned that we need that money for employee training. What are our options?" This will engage your colleague in problem solving, which is inherently collaborative instead of combative.

- **Use hypotheticals.** Being contradicted doesn't feel very good, so don't try to tit-for-tat your counterpart, countering each of his arguments. Instead, says Davey, use hypothetical situations to get him imagining. "Imagining is the opposite of defending, so it gets the brain out of a rut," she says. She offers this example: "I hear your concern about getting the right salespeople to pull off this campaign. If we could get the right people . . . what could the campaign look like?"

Watch your body language— and your counterpart's

The words coming out of your mouth should match what you're saying with your body. Watch your facial expression and what you do with your arms, legs, and entire body. A lot of people unconsciously convey nonverbal messages. Are you slumping your shoulders? Rolling your eyes? Fidgeting with your pen?

Increase your awareness of the energy you give off. In Amy Jen Su and Muriel Maignan Wilkins's book, *Own the Room,* they offer six places where nonverbal messages are communicated through body language: your posture; eye contact; the natural gestures you make typically with your hands; the tone, tempo, and timing of your voice; your facial expressions; and how you occupy the space around you (see table 6-1).

Through each of those points, you signal to others what you're thinking and feeling. Jen Su and Maignan Wilkins use the acronym CENTER to help people remember these six cue points. Table 6-1 shows different signals you might be sending depending on whether you're in an aggressive, conflict-seeking mode or a more passive, conflict-avoidant mode. Reviewing the table and considering the questions will help you maintain body language that's as open as the language you're using.

During your conversation, pay attention to each of these areas and take stock of the overall impression you're giving. Do the same for your counterpart. Watch what she's conveying through her body language. Again, her nonverbal cues may be sending a different message than what she's articulating. If that's the case, or if you're noticing any body language, ask about it. For example, you might say, "I hear you saying that you're fine with this approach, but it looks as if maybe you still have some concerns. Is that right? Should we talk those through?"

Change the tenor of the conversation

Sometimes, despite your best intentions and all of the time you put into preparing for the conversation, things veer off course. You can't demand that your counterpart hold the discussion exactly the way you want.

If things get heated, don't panic. Take a deep breath, mentally pop out of the conversation as if you're a fly on the wall, and objectively look at what's happening.

TABLE 6-1

Manage your body language during a conflict

	What others see when you're avoiding conflict	What others see when you're being aggressive	Questions to ask yourself to keep your body language open
Core posture	• Slouched, loose posture	• Propped, tense, wound-up posture	• What happens to your core posture? Are you standing tall? Slouching?
Eye contact	• Not holding eye contact	• Intense eye contact	• Do you hold eye contact or lose it?
Natural gestures	• Nervous gestures, fidgeting	• Using aggressive gestures like finger-pointing	• What gestures do you start to make? What do you do with your shoulders, hands, and feet?
Tone, tempo, timing	• High pitch or soft volume • Use of filler words such as um, ahs, or stutters	• Fast pace or loud volume • Judgmental or condescending tone	• How does the tone, tempo, and timing of your speech change?
Expressions of the face	• Wide, deer-in-headlights eyes	• Furrowed brows	• What expressions do you make with your face?
Regions and territory	• Shrinks down, doesn't take up space or fill the room	• Takes up too much space at the table or in the room	• How do you take up space in the room?

Source: Adapted from Amy Jen Su and Muriel Maignan Wilkins, *Own the Room: Discover Your Signature Voice to Master Your Leadership Presence* (Boston: Harvard Business Review Press, 2013).

You might even describe to yourself (in your head) what's happening: "He keeps returning to the fact that I yelled at his team yesterday." "When I try to move the conversation away from what's gone wrong to what we can do going forward, he keeps shifting it back." "Every time I bring up the sales numbers, he raises his voice."

Then state what you're observing in a calm tone. "It looks as if whenever the sale numbers come up, you raise your voice." Suggest a different approach: "If we put our heads together, we could probably come up with a way to move past this. Do you have any ideas?"

"Stepping back and explicitly negotiating over the process itself can be a powerful game-changing move," says Weiss. If it seems as if you've entered into a power struggle in which you're no longer discussing the substance of your conflict but battling over who is right, step back and either return to your questions above or talk about what's not working. Say, "We seem to be getting locked into our positions. Could we return to our goals and see if we can brainstorm together some new ideas that might meet both our objectives?" See the sidebar "Phrases That Productively Move the Conversation Along." Returning your counterpart to his original goal may be enough to get the conversation back on track.

When to Bring in a Third Party

There are times, however, when you're getting nowhere with your counterpart and, even when you follow the principles above, you're still not able to have a productive discussion. Some problems are too entrenched, complicated, or emotional to sort out between two people. Or

PHRASES THAT PRODUCTIVELY MOVE THE CONVERSATION ALONG

- "You may be right, but I'd like to understand more."

- "I have a completely different perspective, but clearly you think this is unfair, so how can we fix this?"

- "Can you help me make the connection between this and the other issues we're talking about?"

- "I'd like to give my reaction to what you've said so far and see what you think."

- "I'm sensing there are some intense emotions about this. When you said 'X,' I had the impression you were feeling 'Y.' If so, I'd like to understand what upset you. Is there something I've said or done?"

- "This may be more my perception than yours, but when you said 'X,' I felt . . ."

- "Is there anything I can say or do that might convince you to consider other options here?"

your counterpart is too inflexible or unable to hear your side, insisting that it's her way or the highway.

The main indicator you may need outside help, says White, is when it seems as if your counterpart is perpetuating the conflict rather than trying to solve it. "She may be alternatively conciliatory and antagonistic. Every time you seem to be making progress, she walks back from the tentative agreement and accuses you of not negotiating in good faith," she explains.

This is not a failure. "Someone who is not involved in the conflict may be able to provide vital perspective for both parties," says Gerzon. Ideally, you'll both agree that a third party is necessary before going with this option. But if you can't reach agreement on anything else, this might be difficult. In these cases, you may have to ask someone else to get involved without your counterpart's permission.

Who you bring in will depend on the nature of the conflict. Choose someone whom you both trust and can rely on to understand the issues but also brings an outside perspective. It might be one or both of your bosses. "For example," says Ben Dattner, "if roles are poorly defined, a boss might help clarify who is responsible for what." If the conflict is over how people are rewarded, you might turn to HR or a union representative. Dattner shares another example: "If incentives reward individual rather than team performance, HR can be called in to help better align incentives with organizational goals."

When you've exhausted all your internal options, or if there is no one to appeal to, you might need a trained mediator to help.

In the process of having a productive discussion with your counterpart—expressing your point of view and listening to hers—a resolution may naturally arise. It may be that there was a misunderstanding and now it's cleared up. Or perhaps after hearing your colleague out, you realize you do agree with how she's approaching the project. Or as you talk through what her goals are, you stumble upon a solution that would work well for both of you.

If this doesn't happen organically, you'll have to more consciously work toward a resolution that meets both your and your counterpart's goals.

Resolving a Conflict

CHAPTER 7

Get to a Resolution and Make a Plan

When addressing the conflict directly, the final step is to broker a resolution between you and your counterpart. Start by understanding what a resolution looks like. Then with that goal in mind, take steps to narrow down the options and make the final call.

What a Resolution Looks Like

The details of each specific resolution will vary depending on the type of conflict you were having. With task conflict, the resolution is likely to be an agreement about what it is you want to accomplish—the stated objective for the project you're coleading or an agenda for the next managers' meeting. It will be something concrete that you can write down. The same goes for a process conflict.

Ideally you'll be able to document the process you'll use going forward—how to reach consensus before approving new projects or the sequencing for rolling out the IT initiative. With status conflict, the resolution may be reaching an understanding about who will lead a project or whose team is ultimately responsible for the success of the product launch.

Resolutions in a relationship conflict can be the most difficult to broker and recognize, especially because there are usually bruised feelings that take a while to heal. Often you might agree to each do something differently in the future—he will not raise his voice when he disagrees with you, and you will not run to your boss until you've talked with your counterpart first.

But no matter what type of conflict you were engaged in—relationship, task, process, or status—a resolution needs to meet the same three criteria.

It satisfies as many interests as possible

During your conversation, you spent a lot of time and energy explaining your perspective and goals. You also learned about your counterpart's underlying interests. Perhaps she wanted to be sure that her team was well represented at an important presentation so that they had an opportunity to show off their work, while you wanted the presentation to go quickly and smoothly so that there was plenty of time at the end for questions. It's possible—and preferable—that an agreement meets each of those interests reasonably well. "The essence of a resolution is that you get to what the underlying interests are and try to satisfy as many of them as possible," says Jonathan Hughes.

It's fair and reasonable

"We all want a resolution that feels fair and reasonable to everyone involved—and is defensible to others on the outside looking in," says Hughes. You should be able to answer yes to the following questions: "Do I think this is a reasonable solution?" "Does my counterpart?" "Can I defend it to my boss or anyone else who cares about the outcome?" We also want to feel as though we came to the agreement by ourselves and weren't pressured into conceding or giving in. So both the final arrangement and the process you used to reach it need to be fair.

The relationship is intact

If you reach a resolution that meets the business needs and is fair and reasonable, but you end up hating each other, then it's hard to call that a success. You want to be able to say that you maintained your relationship, or that you even improved it. "The icing on the cake is if you can honestly say to each other that you learned something about each other in the process," says Hughes, "and thus that the next disagreement or conflict will be that much easier to resolve together."

How You Reach a Resolution

Arriving at a resolution that meets those three criteria requires additional conversation, and it's up to you and your counterpart to come up with options. Be creative and collaborative as you do that. Then evaluate the options you generated and make the final call together.

Be creative

Keep in mind your goal, and that of your counterpart, and when all the data is on the table, offer different options that ideally meet both of your needs. Are there ways to satisfy both of your interests and build on that to discover new benefits neither one of you envisioned on your own? Consider a salary increase. You may be fighting for a 10% raise, while your boss thinks you deserve 7%. Instead of just duking it out over the exact percentage, find a way to include something in the raise that's valuable to both of you. Perhaps you can take on a new project for your region that allows you to travel and get exposure to more senior leaders. Taking a creative approach to the conflict, instead of focusing on and nitpicking over a number, increases what you can both get out of it.

Don't get locked into your answer and his answer. Proposing several alternatives helps the other person see a way out, and it also signals humility, that you don't believe there's just one way to resolve this dispute: your way. Don't offer what you originally came to the table with, but use the information you gathered during your conversation to come up with a better solution. There are always additional ways of solving a problem. "When you're creative about how to meet your interests, you can begin to imagine a third way that might meet your needs well and work for both of you," says Hughes.

Be collaborative

Brainstorm possibilities together. If you propose a potential solution, ask for your counterpart's input. Ask, "What other ideas might you have?" and let him build on your ideas or offer others. When you suggest a potential resolution, don't just say, "Do you like it?" but invite criticism. Weiss suggests you ask "What would be wrong with this solution?" That better helps you understand his viewpoint and encourages him to also be creative.

Consider what you can offer

If you've proposed a solution that potentially puts the other person in a difficult spot or takes something away from her, ask yourself: Is there something I can give back? says Holly Weeks. If, for instance, you're telling your boss that you can't take on a particular assignment, propose a viable alternative, such as someone else who can fill the role equally well. "Be constructive," says Jean-François Manzoni. Or if you're laying off someone you've worked with for a long time, "you could say, 'I have written what I think is a strong recommendation for you; would you like to see it?'"

Decide how to evaluate the possibilities

With several options on the table, begin evaluating them. Agree on the criteria you'll use to select the best option. Perhaps you'll ask a disinterested third party to weigh in on your resolution and see if it looks fair. Or maybe you'll agree on certain requirements that the resolution must meet, such as mitigating the risk of a lawsuit or being cost-effective. "It's often easier to agree on the criteria than the solution," says Hughes. These can be hard to establish in a relationship conflict, however. In those situations, fairness is usually the standard against which to evaluate possibilities.

This may all sound rational and reasonable, and maybe collaborating on a resolution will be exactly that. But just as emotions were a key element of the conflict up to this point, they're likely to be present in this part of the conversation as well. Continue to remain calm, acknowledge and label your feelings, and allow for venting when necessary. All the tips you learned for having a productive conversation in the previous chapter will continue to be useful here.

Make the final call

Often with task, process, and status conflict, there is a tangible decision to make. Are we going to finish this project in six months or one year? Can we fund this project and at the same time put a small amount of money toward another one that we'll plan to fully fund next year? Using the criteria you've laid out and the options you've developed, you and your counterpart must agree on which path to pursue and under which arrangements. Other times there is no decision to make, especially with relationship conflict. In those cases, "sometimes just talking it through will resolve it," says Hughes. Once you understand your counterpart's perspective, you may not feel so bad about the way he spoke to you in that meeting. And once he sees that you misinterpreted his reaction, he may be more forgiving of the fact that you left the room before the meeting was over. "No one's at fault," says Hughes. "No one's the bad guy. And accepting that can take the sting out of the fight."

Document the agreement

This doesn't have to be formal, such as a contract. Capture your discussion in an email and send it with a quick note that asks, "Did I get this right?" Confirming what you've agreed to ensures you're on the same page and gives you both something to refer to should any similar issues arise again. You want to do this as soon after your conversation as possible—definitely within a day or two. Leaving it any longer risks that you'll misremember what you both agreed to.

When to Accept That There Won't Be a Resolution

There are some situations in which, try as you might, you won't reach a resolution. You've engaged in a constructive discussion and come up with alternatives for resolving the particular conflict you're having, but you can't make the final call on which option to go with. It may be that your counterpart insists on one solution and you're unwilling to go with that one. Perhaps you have your heart set on a particular option, but it doesn't meet your counterpart's interests. Be realistic with yourself about what's possible so that you don't bang your head against the wall trying to force a solution when there isn't one.

If you can't reach a resolution, there are three things you can do:

- **Take a break.** Sometimes, if you step away from the conversation, let the emotions cool down a little, and return to it later, you might see a different option neither of you thought of before or an existing possibility may look more appealing to one or both of you. This is an especially good tactic if you feel bullied into accepting an outcome. "When someone threatens us, we tend to make irrational decisions, so we need time to figure out whether this is, in fact, something we are willing to accept, or whether it's worse than no agreement," says Judith White. "This will give you the time to consider the offer and save you from one of three mistakes: accepting something you should have rejected; rejecting something you should have accepted, or blowing up at the other person and thereby blowing up any hope of a mutually agreeable solution."

- **Appeal to someone more senior.** You can escalate the situation to a person in a higher position. You might say to your boss or your counterpart's boss, "We're in this fix and we need your help to make the decision." You might ask that person to "decide for the two of you, to intervene and offer another solution, or to change one of the constraints, such as giving you more resources or extending a deadline," explains Hughes.

- **Get your needs met another way.** In lieu of settling your conflict, what can you do instead? If you and a supplier disagree on the terms of your contract renewal, can you find another supplier? Or stay with this supplier, but escalate the conflict to his boss? Or you could hold out for a few months and see if the deal gets better with time. If you're in a dispute about how much of a raise you'll get, and it doesn't look as if HR is going to give you what you asked for, can you look for a different job or go freelance?

Learn from Your Experience

Once you've reached a successful conclusion, it's worthwhile to reflect and consider what went well and what didn't, says Manzoni. "Why did you have certain reactions, and what might you have said differently?" Weeks also recommends observing how others successfully cope with these situations and emulating their tactics. The goal is to constantly improve your approach to conflict by integrating new tactics and strategies. Talk with your boss, a mentor, or a trusted colleague about what you've learned and ask them to remind you and hold you accountable so that you don't repeat the same mistakes.

It's also a good time to talk with your counterpart about what you'll do if you enter into a conflict again. What do each of you want to do differently? How can you make sure that future disagreements don't turn ugly? Document these ideas (again an email is fine) so that you can both refer back to them if you need to.

Once the content of the disagreement has been solved, think about what other reparations you might need to make. Even if your dispute was purely task related or process related, be mindful that your relationship may have suffered. Restoring trust and accepting the situation are critical parts of moving on.

CHAPTER 8

Repair the Relationship

Whether you're shaking hands after a productive conversation, carrying on business as usual, returning to your desk knowing someone intervened on your behalf, trying to accept that there will be no resolution, or plotting how to find an entirely new job, it's important to put the conflict behind you and move on. And even if you've come to an agreeable resolution, sometimes the relationship needs to be mended. There may be some lingering resentment or you or your counterpart may be anxious that the situation will happen again.

If you opted to do nothing, you still need to think about the relationship. You don't want to harbor negative feelings toward the person, especially if you were the one who decided against other options for addressing the disagreement. "You need to tell yourself: 'I chose to let this go. I'm not going to ruminate or retaliate because it was my decision to let go,'" says Jeanne Brett. Even if you didn't make the decision about how to handle the situation, it's still in your best interest to move past it.

Putting your relationship back on track requires addressing your needs, those of your counterpart, and those of the people who may have been party to the conflict.

Pause and Reflect

You might feel amped from the tension even after it's been resolved, or plain exhausted from the mental gymnastics of trying to remain calm, listen, and balance your goals with your counterpart's all at the same time. Or perhaps you're worn out from working hard to let the conflict go. No matter what you're feeling, take a moment to consider what you've accomplished: Not only did you make it through the conflict in one piece, but you made smart choices about how to handle it, remained flexible, and pushed yourself to stay present. Well done. Now consider taking a break from work. After a heated discussion, you may want to take a walk outside, go to the gym, or meet up with a friend. Or you may just want to go home and get a good night's sleep. Chances are that with a little time and space, any lingering negative energy will dissipate and you'll return to work feeling clearer and more focused.

Look Forward

Although you'll want to reflect and learn from what happened, resist the tendency to analyze every detail of the conflict. Who said what? Why did they say it? That isn't productive. "Lots of people think that it's only by understanding the past that we get beyond it. But what you focus on is what grows," Susan David says. So contemplate what's worked well previously, what you like about the person, and what you want from the relationship. "Take a solution-focused approach, not a diagnostic one," she says. (See the sidebar "A Success Story" for one example of how a common purpose helped two people move beyond their conflict.)

Rebuild Rapport

If the relationship has suffered some damage, don't expect it to change overnight. "The real shifts in relationships happen less in those watershed moments and more in your everyday actions," David explains. Sitting down and talking is helpful, "but that's not where the work really happens. It's more subtle than that." Make an effort to change the tone of your everyday interactions. Say hello before you sit down at your desk in the morning. Offer to buy him a coffee. Small gestures of civility go a long way.

Reconnect Through Questions

One way to rebuild rapport is to ask questions, says Caroline Webb, author of *How to Have a Good Day: Harness the Power of Behavioral Science to Transform Your Working Life*. "It's inherently rewarding to people to get to talk about themselves or share their opinions." The trick is to move beyond more typical, factual questions like "When's the presentation due?" to what Webb calls "quality questions" that go beyond exchanging basic information. Instead of asking "How was your weekend?"

A SUCCESS STORY

Rachel had an ongoing conflict with her coworker, Pia. At the consultancy where they worked, it was Rachel's job to sell projects to clients, but it was Pia's role as the business director to vet the sales proposals and pricing. Whenever Rachel sent Pia a draft for review, Pia would increase the prices that Rachel was pitching. She'd send back a curt email that explained the prices were too low and told Rachel to fix them, which Rachel did. As a result, Rachel lost potential sales.

Because she didn't know Pia personally (she had met her only once at a team retreat), Rachel went to her boss, the regional manager, to explain that Pia was being unreasonable about the prices and rude to her. "I had targets I was supposed to meet, and every time Pia caused me to lose a sale, I was getting angrier and angrier," Rachel says. But Rachel's boss was not receptive to her appeals. "She told me that she trusted Pia's judgment implicitly and that I just had to find clients who were willing to pay the premium price," she says.

The circumstances were starting to affect Rachel's morale, not to mention her sales performance. She didn't enjoy going to work anymore because she wasn't making progress toward her goals. She cringed every time she got an email from Pia. One day, after learning that she'd lost yet another potential sale, she called Pia.

Rather than criticize her, though, Rachel explained how upset she was and the impact the situation was having on her: "I wanted to let her know that I really couldn't keep working like this, having strained relationships with my colleagues, bringing in clients and losing them again and again."

Pia was receptive to what she had to say. "She heard me out and said she wasn't aware of how she was coming across." It turned out that Pia was also frustrated by the lack of sales and her performance was also being affected. "This gave us a common purpose to address," Rachel says. So the two of them switched into problem-solving mode. How could they both do their jobs and close the deals together? "She taught me how she did the pricing, and we reached a compromise on what could be quoted," Rachel says.

Pia and Rachel ended up closing several big deals together. "We weren't best buds, but we didn't have any further disagreements either," she says. Both women eventually left the company, but they still keep in touch.

ask what your counterpart did specifically and follow up with something like, "That's interesting. What led you to do that?" If you don't have a personal relationship, ask questions that signal you value his opinion: "How did you think that meeting went?" "What are you working on at the moment?" The goal with these questions is to create what Susan David calls "a shared psychological space." Make it less about you and more about "creating a connection," she advises.

Reestablish Reciprocity

You'll also want to restore trust if it was broken. One smart way to do that, Brian Uzzi says, is to "offer things to the other person without asking for anything in return." Propose taking on a small project she hasn't been able to get to. Or bring her lunch one day. This will activate the law of reciprocity and restore the give-and-take of your previous relationship. But don't verbalize what's taking place. "That will get you into the tight accounting system of who's doing what for whom," warns Uzzi. Keep your word, too. "Being true to the things you've offered will continue to deepen the relationship and make sure it doesn't slip back into mistrust," says Uzzi.

Apologize

"You don't have to be completely at fault to say you're sorry or show some penance," says Adam Galinsky. It's rare that a conflict is completely one-sided, so chances are that you contributed to the situation in some way. Apologize for your part and express genuine regret that the situation occurred (only if you feel it). Doing this will often elicit a similar expression from your counterpart. But don't expect that. You don't want to resent the person if she doesn't apologize, too.

Focus on Commonalities

During the course of your conflict, you likely had disagreements that emphasized how different you were from one another. This can push you apart. Webb says that "if we see someone as part of our in-group, we're more likely to feel empathy for them and not see them as a threat." And fortunately, "it takes very, very little to perceive someone is like you." Find something you agree on. Perhaps it's the common ground you identified before your discussion or something as simple as a shared dislike of the new printer. If this is someone you've had a long-standing relationship with, talk about projects you've worked on together that went well. Reminisce about things you've done in the past. Consider paying the person a compliment or asking about his pet. "Flattery—no matter how ludicrous it is—always works," says Webb.

Spend More Time Together

"One of the best ways to repair a relationship is to work on a project that requires coordination," says Bob Sutton, a Stanford University management professor. This seems counterintuitive, since you may be sick of each other at this point. "Over time, if you work together closely, you may come to appreciate your colleague more and perhaps even develop some empathy," he says. You may discover there are reasons for your counterpart's actions: stress at home, pressure from his boss, or maybe he's tried to do what you're asking for and failed. Spending more time with him will also grant you the opportunity to have more-positive experiences.

Involve Other People

It's likely that throughout the conflict, you turned to other people for advice and commiseration. Your attempts to repair the relationship won't be successful if those people aren't included. "You need to get any involved third parties on board to fix it and keep it healthy," says Uzzi. Explain to your confidants that you're working on the relationship and that you'd appreciate their support in making it work. You might say: "I know Howard and I have been at odds over the past few weeks, and you've heard an earful from me. I want to let you know that we've sorted through our problems, and I'm determined to make our relationship work. It'd be great if you could help by calling me out if I start to complain again." This helps not only you but those around you as well. You're contributing to an office or team culture that allows for conflict to happen. "You're showing that it's safe to disagree," says Annie McKee. "It's not enough to deal with conflict well; you have to make sure everyone knows it was dealt with well."

Consider Providing Feedback

This isn't always possible, but if you've directly addressed the conflict and you've reached a resolution, you might want to give your colleague some feedback about the process. You can share observations with the intention of improving how you interact in the future. It may be that how your counterpart behaved with you is something that regularly gets in her way as a professional. "Don't assume the person knows how she is coming across," says Sutton. This isn't a diatribe about everything she did to annoy you—that will just pull you back into the fray. Focus on behaviors that she can control. Describe how they affected you and your work together with the aim of supporting change. Your carefully framed feedback can help her develop greater self-awareness and increase her effectiveness. And of course, you also need to be open to hearing feedback yourself. If you're seeing some things that your counterpart might change, she's liable to have her own observations to share with you.

However, weigh this option carefully. Daniel Goleman, author of *Emotional Intelligence: Why It Can Matter More Than IQ*, says whether you give feedback "depends on how artful you are as a communicator and how receptive they are as a person." If you feel your counterpart might be open and you can have a civilized conversation, then go ahead. But if this is a person you suspect will be vindictive or mad, or will turn it into a personal conflict, don't risk it. You'll be back to where you started.

For most of us, the word *conflict* conjures up a difficult struggle: We want people to like us, but we also want to get our way. It would be ideal if our colleagues always saw the brilliance in our ideas, gave us the resources we asked for, completely agreed with us on the best way to run the business, *and* still adored us at the end of the day. But work is not a perfect place. Fortunately, it doesn't have to be. And when we fight with people at work, it doesn't have to be scary or threatening. "Going through difficult experiences can be the makings of the strongest, most resilient relationships," says David. We make it through, and in the process, we learn about each other, and ourselves, as we make the next conflict less likely to occur or at least easier to manage.

CHAPTER 9

Navigate Common Situations

For every conflict you encounter, you'll tweak your approach depending on the circumstances. But there are some specific situations that commonly occur.

This chapter will walk you through the following challenges:

- You're fighting from afar

- Your counterpart is passive-aggressive

- Your colleague goes over your head

- You're caught in the middle of two warring colleagues

- You're mad at your boss

- You're dealing with a bully

- Your counterpart is suffering from a mental illness

- You manage two people who hate each other

- Your team turns on you

- You're fighting with someone outside the office

Knowing a bit more about why these situations happen can help you to better tackle them.

You're Fighting from Afar

The situation

You're coleading an important project with your London-based colleague, and his emails have turned snarky. You were initially debating when the project should launch, but now he's sending you emails with just a "?" in them if you don't respond within the hour. Since you're based in Hong Kong, that means you'd have to be up at midnight to receive his "urgent" 5 p.m. emails. He seems really mad, but who can tell, since you're just reading his words on a screen.

Why it happens

"Task-related disputes can more quickly devolve into relationship conflicts when there's no face-to-face contact, which helps to accelerate empathy," says Keith Ferrazzi, who studies virtual teams. A study by Syracuse's Kristin Byron showed that using email generally increases the likelihood of conflict and miscommunication. Cultural differences may also be contributing to the problem if you and your colleague are from different countries.

What to do about it

"The good news is that bad relationship conflicts don't occur as often because virtual team members are typically focused more on their work and less on interpersonal issues and office politics. Hence, bad blood is less likely to develop between coworkers," explains Ferrazzi. Still, it can be harder to solve these conflicts when they do arise because you don't know how the other person is reacting. Is he opting to do nothing and set aside his feelings, or is he actually stewing?

Assess your options

The approaches you might use for navigating conflict take on a different flavor when you work far apart. The do-nothing option can work well when you don't have to see your colleague every day; you may be able to get over the conflict more easily by not addressing it. Or you can indirectly address it by asking someone at your colleague's location to talk with her. Also, exiting the relationship can be easier in these situations because you can ask to work with someone else on the team, or you may be able to go around the person and work with her boss.

Move the conversation to a better medium

As discussed in chapter 5, "Get Ready for the Conversation," arguing through email can be tough, but sometimes that's your only form of communication. "People often behave with far less restraint in a virtual environment than in the physical world—a phenomenon that psychologists call the 'online disinhibition effect,'" says Ferrazzi. And it's just too difficult to interpret what's really going on. If you're arguing via email, stop. Pick up the phone and call your colleague, or schedule a time to do a video call.

Get to know how your counterpart works

Understanding your counterpart—his approach to conflict, his goal in the conversation, and so forth—is central to successfully navigating a conflict. But when you work in different offices, you need to take this task a step further. Do you know how the other person works? Are the tools and processes you use compatible? Pamela Hinds, who studies dispersed teams, says that when people share these kinds of details, or at least an understanding of their contextual differences, there is less conflict. "The challenge on global teams is that the contexts *are* different—that's unavoidable. But we found that as long as team members understand what is different, they're less likely to blame one another for incompatibilities," she says. If possible, visit your colleague's office, and vice versa, to get a sense of how he works. If you can't do that, spend extra time explaining your systems and processes, noting similarities and differences.

Increase informal communication

Research by Mark Mortensen of INSEAD and Hinds also showed that casual, unplanned communication dramatically reduces conflict when you're not in the same location. Take advantage of opportunities for informal interactions. Keep your messaging app open to share personal snippets or jokes throughout the day. Take virtual breaks together, chatting on the phone while you both sip tea. Or you might leave your computer cameras on so that you can see each other throughout the day. "These video links between offices create a shared space and provide more opportunities for these spontaneous—but often very productive—workplace conversations," says Mortensen.

Diane's story

Diane started a new job in the US office of an international NGO. After several weeks of building a rapport over email with Brigitte, a German colleague—and believing that they had started a friendship—Diane got an email from Brigitte that said, "People here in Europe are saying that you're not right for your job." Diane was hurt and assumed that her colleague didn't like her. Why else would she say something so mean and in such an abrupt way? But she didn't want to jump to conclusions, especially since she'd never met Brigitte in person. Diane didn't know anyone in Brigitte's office to turn to for advice or insights into Brigitte's style or personality. She opted to do nothing, ignore the email, and move on, but after a few days, it was still bothering her. She set up a Skype video call with Brigitte.

When the two connected, Diane was surprised to see Brigitte smiling at her. Diane carefully broached the subject of the email. "I told her I was taken aback by it because I thought we had been getting along well," she says. Brigitte explained that it was precisely because they were establishing a relationship that she'd told Diane about what others were thinking. "She thought she was helping me, giving me information that would be useful as I tried to prove myself in the new role. She did it so directly because that was an appropriate way to communicate in her culture, but I just misinterpreted her intentions," Diane says. The two women started turning on Skype when they got to the office and would chat throughout the day. It also gave others in the European office a way to get to know Diane better as they'd stop by Brigitte's desk to wave or say hello to Diane.

Your Counterpart Is Passive-Aggressive

The situation

Your colleague says one thing in a meeting but then does another. She passes you in the hallway without saying hello and talks over you in meetings, but when you ask to speak with her about it, she insists that everything's fine and the problem is all in your head.

Why it happens

It's not uncommon for colleagues to make a passive-aggressive remark once in a while over a particularly sensitive issue or when they're not sure how to directly address an issue. But persistent passive-aggressive behavior that manifests itself in a variety of situations is a different ball game. These individuals can be self-centered at best and narcissistic at worst, says Annie McKee. "These are people who will often do anything to get what they need, including lie." But it may not be all her fault, either. In many organizations, direct, overt disagreement is not allowed, so "some people have been trained to be passive-aggressive by their cultures," she explains.

What to do about it

Passive-aggressive people are not necessarily more engaged in conflict than most, but they're doing it in a way that's tough to deal with. It's not as clean as the indirect approach described in chapter 2, "Your Options for Handling Conflict," because they're not being honest about their intentions. "Fighting with these people is like shadowboxing," says McKee. It's best to do nothing and work around them or to distance yourself (exit), if possible. Also, try the following suggestions.

Accept that your counterpart's behavior likely has nothing to do with you

It's not in your head; it's in hers. Recognize the behavior for what it is, says McKee, but don't spend too much time psychoanalyzing her. Amy Jen Su and Muriel Maignan Wilkins say, "You need all the energy you can muster as a leader, so don't waste an ounce of it trying to figure out why she acts this way with you."

See through the behavior to the source of the conflict

Instead of harping on how much she bothers you, focus on what's causing the disagreement. Does she think that the way you're running the project isn't working (process conflict), but she hasn't directly said that? Or do you disagree about whether your team's ultimate goal is to increase revenue or boost brand recognition (task conflict)? As discussed in chapter 1, "Types of Conflict," knowing what's underneath the disagreement can help to depersonalize it, and when passive-aggressive behavior makes everything feel like a relationship conflict, understanding and labeling the real source can help you move forward.

Focus on a common goal

You've thought about what your goal is and what you suspect hers to be, but her behavior may prevent you from establishing common ground. Instead, focus on the objective you share with others, suggests McKee. If your project is at risk of not getting completed on time, that's the problem you need to deal with, not her infuriating conduct. Sure, you may be tempted to vent with others who also work with her, but limit those conversations. They aren't professional or productive. After a few minutes of complaining, redirect the discussion to your work. You might say: "Enough about her. Let's talk about how we can get this project done."

Enlist help from others

Amy Jen Su and Muriel Maignan Wilkins suggest you enroll your team in keeping your passive-aggressive colleague accountable. Have others confirm expectations that you agreed on. "For example," they explain, "if you're in a meeting discussing next steps, make sure everyone articulates what they heard and verbally communicates what they commit to in specific terms (not just head nodding)." Or you can send a follow-up email documenting who's going to do what. "Form an esprit de corps with your other colleagues," suggests McKee. And since your colleague is passive-aggressive with everyone, politely ask others what coping mechanisms or tactics work for them.

Darrell's story

Darrell's new coworker, Raquel, was turning out to be a nightmare. Their boss had asked Darrell to show Raquel how to complete several reports that she'd eventually be responsible for, and when he sat down with her, she acted like she already knew how to do them. "It was impossible since the reports were specific to our organization, but when I tried to point that out, she told me to not get so worked up," he says. "That was the first sign that something was wrong."

One day, Darrell overheard her telling their boss that she was still waiting for him to train her on the reports. He didn't want to get defensive in front of his manager, so instead he went to Raquel and tried to appeal to their shared goal. "I told her that we both wanted her to be able to take over the reports," he says. He again offered to show her, but she told him that she had it under control. Since the direct approach wasn't working, he decided to go to their boss. "It wasn't what I wanted. I really hoped I could work it out with her, but she acted like nothing was wrong every time I tried to address it," he says. Darrell explained his side to the boss. "I didn't ask him to talk to her because I thought that would make matters worse, but I wanted him to know that what she was saying wasn't true."

Darrell was extremely frustrated, but he didn't see a way out of the situation. He had to work with Raquel, and she wasn't changing her behavior. So he took the do-nothing option and didn't address it further, except to calmly explain his side of the story whenever Raquel told their boss a lie about him. "Luckily for me, I wasn't the only one whom she treated poorly. Two other people in our department noticed the same kind of thing, so we were able to commiserate," he says. None of them figured out a way to get Raquel to stop lying, but they all learned to laugh at the absurdity of her behavior. "I had a choice to be angry at work every day or to shrug her off." Happily for Darrell, Raquel stayed at the company for only a year.

Your Colleague Goes over Your Head

The situation

Your coworker comes to you with a new initiative and asks for your help. You agree that his idea is worthwhile but explain that you just don't have the time or resources to tackle it this quarter. After your conversation, he goes behind your back to share his brilliant idea with your boss. When your manager comes to you to ask why you're not helping your coworker, you're embarrassed and infuriated. Not only has your coworker undermined your authority, now your boss is questioning your decisions.

Why it happens

There are both practical and psychological reasons why a colleague might try to sidestep you. Practically speaking, he may want a different answer or outcome than you've given him. Psychologically, it's possible that he wants to show that he has more clout or authority than you do.

What to do about it

You may be tempted to stomp over to the person's desk and read him the riot act. "You have to be a saint to not be annoyed or stressed or nervous about something like this happening," says Caroline Webb. But, as with any conflict, even one where you feel you've been slighted, it's better to take a more measured approach. Keep in mind that some people don't know that going over your head may be frowned upon. In some cultures, it's not. So don't make assumptions about the person's intentions. Instead, try the following approaches.

Question your assumptions

To help you keep your cool, Webb suggests you start by sorting through what you actually know. You may think your coworker went over your head but that's not necessarily true. Ask yourself what the facts of the situation are and try to strip your explanation of emotional language. Rather than thinking, "He completely disregarded my authority to get a different answer from my boss," tell yourself, "He had a conversation with my boss about his initiative." Focus on what you know. And then ask yourself: What would be different ways to explain this situation? One might be that your coworker is just out for himself, but another could be that your boss asked him what exciting projects he was working on next quarter. "Work out three or four different scenarios," suggests Webb, "that broaden your aperture and help you question the assumption that they've been dastardly or ill-intended."

Find out more

As you think about what you know, also consider what you don't know. If you just heard about the conversation through the rumor mill, find out what really happened. You might go to your boss and ask in a neutral way about what transpired: "Hey, I heard you and Carlos were talking about his new idea." Take care to maintain a casual, nonaccusatory tone so that your boss doesn't think you're trying to start a feud.

Approach your colleague

If after gathering additional facts, you decide to directly address the issue, start with your coworker. You'll likely need to have a conversation with your boss, too (more on that later), but that discussion will go better if you can report on how you handled things with your colleague. Ask your coworker if you can talk—preferably in a private room. Keep an open mind as you enter the conversation, says Adam Galinsky. This is true anytime you directly address a conflict, but especially in a situation like this when you likely feel put upon or upset. Remember your goal, whether it's to have a strong working relationship, to restore trust, or to protect your time. Don't go into the conversation with the intention of sticking it to your coworker. That's just going to set you up for a battle. Instead, be open to hearing what he has to say about the situation and why he did what he did.

State what you know and how you feel

Begin by saying what you know and how it made you feel. "Make it a straightforward discussion," says Galinsky. Let the person know that you're disappointed by what he did but stay away from words like "angry" or "betrayed." That may be how you feel, but it's going to put your coworker on the defensive, advises Webb. Instead say: "I heard you talked to Roger about your initiative after we discussed it and that made me feel a bit concerned that we're not communicating well."

Problem-solve, together

Once you've shared what you know and heard his perspective, decide together how to remedy the situation. "Try asking them for their thoughts first, before building on their suggestions. Research shows that people feel far more attachment to any idea that they've had a hand in shaping," explains Webb. So instead of saying, "Here's how we should handle this situation," ask, "What do you think would be the best way to address this, given where we are now?" Once you've agreed on how to rectify the current issue, discuss how you'll handle similar situations in the future.

Clarify the lines of communication

Ideally, you'll both agree that your coworker should come directly to you next time and then actually follow through on that. But if he's not on board with that plan, prevent this situation from recurring by showing him that going over your head won't be effective. Make clear that you and your boss are in regular contact and if he

133

goes to your manager, you're going to find out. You might say something along the lines of, "I meet with Roger regularly to discuss our group's priorities and he usually lets me know if he gets requests from other teams." You don't need to say this in a threatening way; think about it as educating him on the lines of communication.

Repair your relationship with your boss

You may be ticked off that your boss didn't redirect your colleague to you and wonder if he has faith in your judgment. And this breach in the chain of command may have also annoyed your boss or caused him to question your ability to do your job. So once you've settled things with your colleague, talk with your boss about what happened, why it happened, and how to avoid similar situations in the future. Start by considering what you want to get out of the conversation. Webb suggests you may "want to come off as wise, thoughtful, and in control." Your goal here may be to restore your reputation or to re-establish ground rules for communication. Then lay out what you know (for a fact) and how it made you feel: "I heard that Carlos talked to you about his initiative and that made me concerned that I might be out of the loop. Can I ask what happened or how you saw it from your perspective?" Then it's your job to listen. Once you've heard his side of things, you might ask, "What can we do differently when this happens in the future?" You can gently suggest that next time your colleague goes to him, he redirect him to you: "If Carlos comes to you again, would you mind sending him to me so we can address the issue without having to take up your time?"

Gina's story

Gina was responsible for helping new employees get up to speed on current processes and best practices for initiating sales with customers. She was training Dante, who had been hired to work with their biggest customer. Dante was more senior than Gina. "I could tell that he wasn't necessarily pleased to be taking direction from me and had a general air about him that told me that he didn't think I could really teach him anything," she says. Dante wasn't happy with the process and timeline that Gina explained the company typically used with customers. He thought it was too strict and wanted to bypass particular parts of the process, such as getting customer signoff before sending initial samples, in order to speed up the sale. So he went to Gina's manager to get approval to ship the samples.

Luckily, Gina's manager reiterated the company's standard process and the reasons behind it. "If he had said yes, it could have completely thrown off our timeline and been a disaster," Gina says. Then the manager had a conversation with Gina about what had happened with Dante.

Gina decided to talk with Dante directly, but she wanted to be careful. "I knew that if I approached him in a certain way, he could easily become defensive and maybe even combative. I didn't want to make any snap judgments about why he did what he did." While she appreciated his desire to move things along more quickly, she also knew that she had insight on why things were done the way they were.

She asked Dante to sit down with her to review the account once more. "I explained the processes thoroughly and stressed how important it was to follow the guidelines—and included the reasoning behind each step," she says. She casually mentioned that their manager had explained what he had tried to do and thanked him for "trying to think outside of the box and see how we could potentially get samples to the customer even faster." She was careful not to make it a huge deal and to focus on the process conflict they were having. "I didn't make it personal," she says. She ended the conversation on a positive note too, offering to help Dante in any way she could. Gina says this approach worked: The two had a great working relationship after that point, and Dante came to her—not their manager—with questions or concerns.

You're Caught in the Middle of Two Warring Colleagues

The situation

Two of your coworkers just don't get along. They exchange mean looks in meetings, and they both come to you to complain about each other. You want to be supportive, but you also don't want to be seen as taking sides.

Why it happens

We all want to have alliances at work—so when two people are having a conflict, it's not uncommon for them to drag other people in. They may want validation of their viewpoint or to demonstrate to the other person that they have more allies. Conflict avoiders often tend to get put in the middle because they generally don't push back when one coworker gossips about another.

What to do about it

When stuck between two adversaries, "people often find themselves in over their head," says Roderick Kramer, of Stanford Graduate School of Business. "They think they can intervene, make suggestions, feel good about themselves, and move the conflict forward in a constructive way. But that's not always possible."

Stay out of it

Whether or not you engage will depend on how enmeshed you already are in the situation. If you feel as if you're being used as a pawn in their war, draw the line and choose to do nothing. This is particularly tough for conflict avoiders to do, but try saying something such as "I'm sorry that you two aren't getting along, but I'd really prefer to stay out of it." If that feels too difficult to do, try to find ways to spend less time with each of them. After you've turned down a coffee break several times, they may get the hint. "Remember that you aren't a psychologist or a mediator," says Kramer. If the situation is outside your comfort zone or you think the disagreement is juvenile, there's nothing wrong with staying out of it. But always give one or both of your coworkers a next step to take. Say, "I'm not sure I'm the right person to help you with this, but you might want to sit down together or with HR."

On the other hand, if you want to lend a sympathetic ear and think you can help them work through it, take the next few steps.

Allow them to vent

It can be hard to listen to people complain about each other, but sometimes that's exactly what they need. By allowing each of them to process the situation with you, they may figure out on their own what the source of their conflict is and how they can sort it out between them. If you're worried that by hearing one person out, you'll upset the other, make an effort to get both sides of the story. Go to the other person and ask, "What's your take on what's going on between you and Harry?" This will give you a fuller picture of the conflict without earning you a reputation as a meddler. It will also equip you to help them solve it.

Empathize

While listening to each colleague, show that you understand how hard the situation is. You can say, "I'm sorry this is happening" or "It's tough when two people can't agree." Stay neutral and speak from your own experience. Offer observations such as, "It seemed as if Jane was stressed out and didn't mean what she said" or "I know that Joe is a direct person and can sometimes come off as harsh." If you're being pushed to choose a perspective, make it clear that you won't: "You seem hurt, but I can't take sides because I have to work with both of you."

Offer advice—cautiously

Before you give your two cents, ask your coworkers if they want your help. "We tend to offer unsolicited advice because we think we know better," says Anna Ranieri, a career counselor and executive coach. But people might not want your opinion, so start by saying something like, "I've observed what's happening between you two. Would it be helpful to hear my take?"

Explain the impact of their fighting

After you've demonstrated your concern, describe how the conflict is affecting the team. Say something like, "You two not getting along is distracting. We've got a lot on our plates right now with the quarter closing soon, so it'd be better if we were focused on getting the reports done." Or "I'm concerned that you're setting a bad example for the younger people on our team. They look up to both of you, and when they see you treating each other this way, they may think it's OK to do the same to others."

Problem-solve together

Just as you would focus on the future if this were your own conflict, help them do the same. Instead of offering concrete suggestions, help them find their own solutions. Ask open-ended questions as discussed in chapter 6, "Have a Productive Conversation." In this situation, those questions might sound more like "How do you hope this will be resolved?" or "What do you want out of your relationship with Greg?" Kramer says, "You should be more in problem-solving mode than gossip mode."

Gary's story

Gary was planning a partner meeting to make decisions about compensation. As the senior partner, it was his job to set the ground rules for the sensitive discussion. Each partner presented his or her accomplishments and progress against goals, then the other partners asked questions, typically polite requests for clarification, before deciding on that partner's bonus for the year. If there was a more serious issue, the partners usually brought it up before the meeting so that it could be addressed outside of this formal setting.

Everyone knew that two partners, Susan and Robert, had been at odds for some time, and each of them came to Gary ahead of time to complain about the other. Susan felt as if Robert wasn't pulling his weight at the firm and his compensation should reflect that. Robert said that Susan was mistreating her team members, especially junior analysts whom she often had stay late at the office for no reason. He wanted her compensation to be affected as well.

Gary heard them both out. He asked that they sort it out between them in advance of the meeting. When they came back a week later even more upset, he suggested that the three of them sit down together and talk about what could be done. He explained that if the two of them couldn't figure out how to stop fighting, they would have to postpone the compensation discussion, which would affect when the bonuses would get paid out. "But I didn't want—and I know they didn't want—to air all of this in front of the larger group," Gary says. He then asked if they wanted to know his opinion. They both said yes. He suggested they should recuse themselves in the discussion of each other's compensation. "That way it was basically a wash for them," he says.

At first, Susan was game and Robert pushed back. "He wanted to say his piece in front of the group," Gary says. But Gary explained to him that the goal of getting the discussion done was more important than his beef with Susan. So when the group met, Susan and Robert sat out for the discussion of each other's performance and compensation. "It was obvious to everyone in the room what was happening and why, but we accepted that because it let us get through the discussion with everyone saving face," he says. Susan and Robert never got along much better, but because they saw that Gary was unwilling to take sides, they stopped appealing to him.

You're Mad at Your Boss

The situation

You did all the work on the unit's big project, but your boss took all the credit. The executive team patted him on the back, and he didn't say a word about the late nights you pulled. You're angry, but you want to broach this sensitive issue with your boss productively.

Why it happens

"Your relationship with your boss is a significant predictor of your experience at work," says Liane Davey. A positive relationship is likely to lead to interesting as-signments, meaningful feedback, and recognition for your contributions, so you want things to go well. But because of that desire, you may also hold your boss to a higher, unobtainable standard.

What to do about it

Fighting with your manager, says McKee, "sparks a deep, primal response: fear." And for good reason. "Bosses hold our lives in their hands—the keys to our futures, not to mention our daily bread." Given that, you could do nothing and move on—as discussed in chapter 2, this is a good option if you don't think your boss will change his ways or is unwilling to hear you. But if you're worried that your anger will only grow, you may want to take the following steps.

Cool down

Remember the advice in chapter 6 about walking away? You don't want to say anything you don't mean. First, give yourself some time—wait a day or two. Your anger may fade to the point where you're willing to let the irk-some behavior go. If not, you may decide to address the conflict directly.

Show respect

This may be the last thing you want to do, especially when you feel slighted, but your boss expects—and hopefully deserves—your respect. You can still label your disagreement as a relationship conflict, but before ex-plaining what's made you so mad, "assure your boss that you respect him and his position," says Joseph Grenny, author of *Crucial Conversations: Tools for Talking When Stakes Are High.* "When that sense of respect is secure, you can venture into expressing your views openly and honestly." You might say, "I enjoy working for you, and I know I have a lot to learn from you."

Focus on the business needs, not yours

When you talk to your boss, you can point out how surprised you were by what he did, but you'll get further with the conversation if you frame it in terms of your goals. What's best for the business? Where do your goals align? Your boss may be more willing to change his behavior if you explain that not sharing the credit could create a bottleneck because those above him think he's the only one who can get things done.

Explain your intent

As you would do any time you address conflict directly, tell your boss what your objective is in giving him this feedback. Do you want to show off the work of the team? Are you concerned that you'll become disengaged if your work isn't recognized? Grenny says that you can clarify your intent by contrasting what you mean with what you don't mean. "I'd like to share a concern, but I'm worried that it will sound as if I doubt your character. I don't. And yet I don't think I'd be fully loyal if I didn't share my perspective. May I do so?"

Alina's story

Alina's company had an informal policy that it wouldn't start work with clients (especially new ones) before there was a signed contract in place. Rodrigo, one of the firm's partners, asked Alina to start working with a new client before he'd gotten the contract finalized. "It was a busy time, and I was stretched incredibly thin, but the project started moving forward pretty quickly," she says. She worked nights and weekends to keep up only to find out that the client pulled out before the contract was signed. Rodrigo sent an email letting Alina and the rest of the team know. It ended with "Sorry about this!" which irked Alina. "It seemed flippant to me, and it was inadequately matched to the suckiness of the situation," she explains.

Rodrigo called her to talk through the logistics of how to wrap up the work, but she didn't feel ready to have the conversation. "I wanted to be prepared, and I was afraid I would talk about how personally annoyed I was when really what bothered me was how much of the firm's money was wasted," she explains. She asked Rodrigo if they could talk the following morning instead. She thought about it that night and decided she wouldn't be able to let it go. Rodrigo might not change, but she really needed to get it off her chest.

She knew that both she and Rodrigo were conflict seekers, so she set up a full hour for them to talk. Then she set the tone for the conversation. "I told him that my pushing back on him was not because I didn't respect him. I did. He was amazing at client service. But I felt as if it would be a disservice to him if I didn't point out why ignoring the policy was so bad." At first, Rodrigo was defensive, arguing about whether or not the contract would've made a difference. After she let him vent, he calmed down and vowed to be better about the contracts in the future. He even asked her to keep him accountable, refusing to do work for him if there wasn't a contract in place.

You're Dealing with a Bully

The situation

Your colleague consistently undermines you in meetings, withholds information you need to do your work, and speaks badly about you. This isn't just one jab on a bad day; it's persistent negative behavior over time. You feel sick to your stomach whenever you see her name in your inbox or hear her voice down the hall.

Why it happens

Research from Nathanael Fast, a professor at the University of Southern California's Marshall School of Business, proves a commonly held idea: People act out when their ego is threatened. "We often see powerful people behave aggressively toward less powerful people when their competence is questioned," he says. It's not just people in positions of authority who act this way. Whoever it is, chances are, she's singled you out for this bullying because she's jealous that others like you or that you have skills she doesn't, says Gary Namie, the founder of the Workplace Bullying Institute. You may also seem like an easy target, particularly if she sees that you shy away from conflict.

What to do about it

Just because you're a victim doesn't mean you can't take action. Try the following.

Understand the situation better

Being bullied can be downright painful. Stepping back and looking at the situation can help give you some insight into the dynamic between the two of you. Are you a conflict avoider while she's a seeker? Are your disagreements mostly relationship conflicts? Or are there elements of task conflict as well? Using the advice in this book can give you some distance from the pain of the situation and the emotional room to start to address it.

Stand up for yourself

Call out bad behavior when it happens. "I believe very strongly in making immediate corrections," says Michele Woodward, an executive coach. "If someone calls you honey in a meeting, say right then: 'I don't like being called that. Please use my name,'" she says. If you're uncomfortable with a direct, public response, Woodward advises saying something as soon as you're able. After the meeting, you could say, "I didn't like being called honey. It demeans me." Show that there is no reward for treating you that way. "The message should be: Don't mess with me; it won't be worth your effort," Namie says.

Enlist help

Talk to colleagues you trust and see what they can do, even if it's simply confirming your perspective. They might stand up for you in a meeting, defending your ideas or asking the bully not to call you honey. Or they might go speak to the bully one-on-one and explain how disruptive her behavior is to the larger group. This can be especially helpful if your supporters have power over the bully or the bully trusts them.

Know the limitations

If your colleagues' interventions don't help, escalate the situation to someone more senior or to HR. Your objective is to get the bullying behavior to stop. But that's not always possible. "The only time I've seen bullies change is when they are publicly fired. The sanctions don't work," says Woodward. Instead, protect yourself. Perhaps take time off from work. Or move on—when you're in an abusive situation at work, the most tenable solution may be to leave, if that's a possibility. The Workplace Bullying Institute has done online surveys that show more people stay in a bullying situation because of pride (40% of respondents) than because of economics (38%). If you're worried about letting the bully win, Namie says, you're better off worrying about your own well-being.

Cedric's story

Cedric took a new position at a veterinary clinic with the intention of buying into the practice, which he did after several months, becoming the business partner of the owner, Ruth. A year later, after what seemed like a minor disagreement, Ruth stopped speaking to Cedric for six weeks. When he confronted her, she told him she was contemplating dropping him as a partner. Cedric was shocked. He had taken out a loan to buy into the firm and felt financially stuck.

Cedric soon recognized a pattern in Ruth's behavior. She was a clear conflict seeker. Any time the two had a conflict, no matter what the original source of the disagreement (task, process), it immediately turned personal. "If I disagreed, she would ice me out. If I confronted her, she iced me out longer," he says. He eventually figured out that stroking her ego was more effective. "You could flatter her, tell her how great she was, how well she did in a case, and she'd be back on your side. I learned to do this sort of dance in order to survive."

But Ruth's harsh behavior wore Cedric down. Things got so bad at one point that she didn't speak to him for three months. He enlisted a professional coach, who helped him see that Ruth was a narcissist and a bully who was threatened by his skills. This gave him the confidence to set his limits: He told her he was looking for someone to buy out his part of the business, and she offered to do it. "It was the best thing I could've done," he says. "I wish I had left when she first showed me who she truly was."

Your Counterpart Is Suffering from a Mental Illness

The situation

You never know what frame of mind you'll catch your fellow team member in. Sometimes when you ask him why he didn't respond to an email you sent, he snaps at you and storms off. Other times, when coworkers challenge his ideas, he laughs inappropriately. When he doesn't show up to meetings or get his share of the team's work done, you're afraid to confront him because you have no idea how he'll react. You wonder whether there's more going on here than just a quirky personality—perhaps he has a mental illness.

Why it happens

In 2014, the National Institute of Mental Health estimated that 18.1% of adults in the United States had a mental illness, most of whom didn't have an official diagnosis. With percentages that high, you're likely to have coworkers with some sort of mental illness—depression, personality disorders, schizophrenia—"especially since many of these issues don't prevent people from working," McKee says.

What to do about it

We can't account for our colleagues' moods, nor should we. "There are clues, however, that let us know that there may be something more going on than a disagreement," says McKee. Your interactions or homework to better understand your counterpart may reveal things such as sudden changes in mood or communication style, personality, or personal habits, or social withdrawal—all of which are indications that your coworker may have an underlying mental health issue. Addressing the conflict could be dangerous—to your and your coworker's well-being. Instead, do the following.

Look for patterns

Is his behavior often erratic? Do his regular actions seem outside the norm? Don't jump to conclusions. "Occasionally people do things that others deem inappropriate, but if it happens on a consistent basis or every time the person feels threatened, it's an indication that there's a larger issue," says McKee.

Don't diagnose

Although it's helpful to recognize when something bigger might be affecting your colleague, don't try to come up with a specific diagnosis. Chances are that you aren't trained to evaluate emotional or psychological problems. "And we really don't know if there's truly something going on," says Judith White. What you can do instead, suggests White, is educate yourself about the symptoms you may be able to observe in family, friends, and colleagues. "The National Alliance on Mental Illness [https://www .nami.org/] is a good resource for friends and family members who either know or suspect mental illness," she says. This information can help you distinguish between an isolated incident that may be safe to address and a deeper problem that is better handled by a professional.

Don't let the problem lie

You might be tempted to steer clear and exercise your do-nothing option because you're afraid or unsure about what to do. Doing nothing may be the right approach to the conflict but not necessarily to the person. It's most certainly a sensitive situation, but that doesn't mean you have to completely ignore it. After all, it may be hard for this person to do his job if he can't get along with people. "Most job descriptions have requirements for 'interaction' or 'collaboration' of some kind baked in, and if the person can't fulfill this aspect of the job, then it's time to step in," says White. Indirectly addressing the conflict is often the right approach here. White recommends asking your boss or HR for help with the problem, or reaching out to your company's employee assistance program, if you have one.

Be compassionate

"Remember that everyone has a story," says McKee. Don't judge what's going on with your colleague. He might be suffering from his behavior as much as or more than you. If you have a close personal relationship and you suspect there is an underlying health issue, gently ask about what might be going on outside of work. But don't push. If he doesn't want to talk, don't force it.

Go by the book

Because of the sensitivity of the situation, this is not a place to wing it. White says to follow any formal rules your company has for resolving the conflict because informal persuasion or negotiation is unlikely to work. "Look up the legal or regulatory rules, and if they don't exist, then find out past precedent in your organization and write it down," says White. Then keep records of your interactions. If the conflict escalates, you'll be able to justify your actions to this person, and to any third parties.

Heather's story

Heather was concerned about her fellow professor, Jacques. "He had always been jovial, but his behavior changed midway through the year," Heather explained. "We were coleading an independent study for five students, and he basically stopped showing up," she says. Every time Heather tried to ask Jacques whether he had read the students' papers or was planning to come to the next meeting, Jacques would snap and insist he was fine. "I felt bad for him, but I was also annoyed because I was picking up his slack and I was already having a busy semester, and here he is yelling at me," says Heather. When she realized that the direct approach wasn't working, Heather thought about doing nothing. She knew that she could cover the class, and she hoped that after the summer break, Jacques might return feeling better. "But that didn't feel right. I didn't want to get him in trouble, but there was clearly something wrong. He had become a different person."

Heather decided to ask for help. She went to their department chair and explained the situation, telling him that some of the students had started to complain. The chair worked with HR to talk with Jacques and convince him to take a leave of absence. Heather found out a year later that Jacques had been suffering from severe depression. "I wasn't surprised, but it explained a lot. I'm glad I handled it the way I did. I tried to be as compassionate as I could."

You Manage Two People Who Hate Each Other

The situation

As a manager you probably didn't expect to play referee, but two of your team members just aren't getting along. They won't look at each other, they openly deride each other, and they refuse to cooperate. How you can right such a dysfunctional relationship?

Why it happens

Conflict, as discussed in chapter 5, is often based on the fear of losing something—ego, respect, status. Your team members may be insecure, anxious about their status in the team, or worried about their jobs. Instead of handling their emotions appropriately, they're taking them out on each other.

What to do about it

You have an obligation to help your team members. You don't have to hold their hands, but you do need to examine your role in the problem and offer suggestions for moving forward.

Hear them out

Give each person a chance to explain his point of view. First, sit down with each person one-on-one. "Redirect comments that include assumptions about what the other person is thinking or feeling," Davey suggests. For example, if he says, "She's trying to destroy my credibility," respond by reframing the idea: "We don't know her motive; I'm interested in how her behavior is being interpreted by you. How do you feel when she disagrees with you in front of the team?"

Determine if you've contributed to the problem

Make sure you haven't set these two up for failure, suggests Davey, by either being unclear about roles or sparking unhealthy competition. Ask: Do they have a clear understanding of what's expected of them? Are their metrics and rewards designed to promote collaboration rather than rivalry? If either answer is no, sit them down to make expectations clear and rejigger their goals so that they can work better together.

Manage your reaction

You may be fed up with these two. If you can't be empathetic, you won't be able to help because your annoyance is likely to further heighten the conflict. "Start with the positive assumption that your direct reports are good people experiencing something stressful," says Davey. This shift in mindset will help in the same way it does when you're addressing your own conflict (as discussed in chapter 5). It will also make you calmer: a key component of managing your emotions—and theirs.

Help them see the other side

Ask questions so that they can understand the other person's perspective. "How do you think she felt when she joined a team of people who are older and more experienced than she is?" "How might you help her get her point across so that she doesn't need to be so assertive?" If there's someone on the team they both get along with, ask that person to serve as a bridge and raise each other's awareness about what the other is thinking.

Bring them together

After they've had a chance to vent and see the situation from the other's perspective, bring them together. Davey suggests you start by saying, "I've been speaking with each of you about my concerns over your strained relationship, and I was hoping you felt ready to talk directly to each other." Interject as little as possible in the conversation, but when you know there is something that's not being said, provide a gentle nudge: "Heather, we talked about your reaction to Tony's tone of voice. Do you want to share that with him?"

Work toward a shared agreement

Ask them each to make commitments about what they'll change. "Heather, what are you planning to do differently going forward? And Tony, how about you?" Then tell them that you'd like to keep them accountable to those promises. Document what they said they would do differently and send it to both of them to confirm agreement.

Focus them on work

Leadership professor Richard Boyatzis says the best way to heal war wounds is to start working again. Give them a relatively easy task to rebuild their confidence as a team. As they restore their relationship, help them follow Bob Sutton's advice from chapter 8, "Repair the Relationship," about working together. Put them on projects that require deeper collaboration and give them the opportunity to work through task or process conflicts.

Prevent additional problems

Encourage your team members to handle issues themselves. Research by Grenny shows that top-performing teams immediately and respectfully confront one another when problems arise. "Not only does this drive greater innovation, trust, and productivity, but it also frees the boss from being the playground monitor," says Grenny. Let new team members know up front that you expect them to hold *you* and others responsible. Call out positive examples and be a good model yourself. If people still come running to you whenever there's a fight, refuse to get involved. If you're not solving it for them, they'll figure out how to do it on their own.

Marshall's story

Marshall, the owner of an eco-lodge, employed four managers including Helga, a German expat who ran the front office and oversaw the staff when Marshall was off-site, and Carlos, a Belizean who was in charge of client services. Helga was incredibly organized and meticulous about her work. Carlos's expertise was client service. "He had an ability to make every guest feel as if he or she is the first one to ever see a snake," says Marshall.

But Helga and Carlos weren't getting along. In fact, Helga asked Marshall to fire Carlos because she felt he wasn't doing his job; he regularly forgot to do tasks and was sloppy with his paperwork. She was frustrated and felt as if she was working twice as hard as he was. Carlos had also previously complained about Helga. He resented her criticism and felt she was too cold to the clients.

As Marshall saw it, they were both failing to understand or appreciate each other's talents. Marshall encouraged Helga to step back and look at the situation.

Carlos was failing to do part of his job description, but he was invaluable to the lodge. Helga conceded that Carlos's job description should be changed so that he could live up to expectations.

He spoke to both employees, explained why each one was extremely valuable to the team, and asked them to appreciate what the other brought. He asked them to focus on the larger purpose and to put their disputes behind them. With expectations reset, Carlos and Helga found a way to work together by accepting that they had completely different styles but both cared ultimately about the same thing—making the lodge successful.

Your Team Turns on You

The situation

Your team members disengage or stop coming to meetings. They simply don't do, or even refuse outright, what you ask of them. They begin meeting without you. You start to worry that you have a mutiny on your hands.

Why it happens

Your team may be upset about a decision you made (or didn't make) or fed up with you continually interrupting them, taking credit for their ideas, or not going to bat for them.

What to do about it

For a leader, this can be a disheartening and terrifying experience, but it's not irreparable. By being open to what's happening, listening to your team, and being direct, you can regain the group's confidence and your effectiveness as a leader.

Find out what's going on

Is one person driving the negativity, or are the feelings shared across the team? Are people taking issue with your leadership, or is fighting among team members causing them to rebel against you? Ask direct and open questions that get at the source of the conflict. It's easiest to do this in one-on-one meetings with team members you trust most. But if they tell you that others have an issue with you, ask them to send the others to talk to you directly.

Name what's happening

Once you've identified the source of the conflict, acknowledge it with your team. "It seems as if you all are upset with the way I've been gathering and incorporating your input into the new strategy. Is that right? Am I missing anything?" Trying to gloss over a problem can turn it into the elephant in the room. "If you're pretending that nothing's wrong and the rest of your team knows there is, it can be really problematic," says Deborah Ancona, an MIT professor. And while you may want to follow the team's lead in not directly addressing the situation, when they're letting the conflict seep out in other ways, doing nothing isn't a smart option.

Own the issue

No matter the cause of the problem, recognize the things that became destructive under your watch. Publicly acknowledge what you have done to contribute to the problem, and explain what you're going to do to address it. "Great leaders are able to get up and say, 'Thanks for the feedback. I realize I haven't been doing X. These are the steps I'm taking to correct this, and I'd appreciate feedback on how it's going,'" says Ancona.

Get outside help if necessary

When a team is particularly defiant or upset, you may not be able to resolve the conflict alone. Find a mediator—either an outside coach or an uninvolved person from another part of the organization—to get the issues out in the open and negotiate a resolution. Typically you do this when you've exhausted all options, as discussed in chapter 7, "Get to a Resolution and Make a Plan," but you may need to go this route sooner because there are so many people involved and you may not get the whole story as the boss. Working with a coach can help you understand why your style or approach is not effective with your team.

Katja's story

Katja was ready to close her marketing company. The business was doing OK, but there were some severe personnel problems: Morale was low, and her employees were angry and resentful. "The soul of my business was black," she recalls.

When she looked honestly at the situation, she saw that there wasn't disagreement over task or process or even status. It was pure relationship conflict. Her boyfriend at the time convinced her to work with an executive coach before she truly called it quits. The coach helped her to develop a plan to address the conflict. She started by talking with members of her staff to find out what was going on. But every time she spoke to anyone, they would claim they didn't have an issue, but someone else did. "Eventually, I started to realize that no one was going to own up to the conflict, so I had to get it out in the open."

Katja requested that they start communicating directly. There couldn't be any gossip if they were going to turn things around and improve their relationships. She also acknowledged her role in creating the destructive atmosphere. She herself had gossiped on occasion, and she knew she'd set a bad example. Once her employees started having the difficult conversations needed to resolve their conflicts with her and with one another, they began to feel more united and committed. Soon they realized there was pent-up client demand they hadn't been able to serve because they were so wrapped up in what was going on inside the business. In the next six years, the company's revenue tripled.

You're Fighting with Someone Outside the Office

The situation

Your vendor has missed several deadlines, and you're getting nervous the IT project isn't going to get done on time. But your contact there isn't answering your calls or emails. You're wondering if it's time to switch vendors.

Why it happens

When you're interacting with people in other organizations—a customer, supplier, a partner—you typically know little about them. Without the shared context of an office, colleagues, and other commonalities, it's easy for you and an external partner to misunderstand each other or misinterpret intentions.

What to do about it

Whether the person is a vendor who has missed several deadlines, a customer who complains about a rise in your product's price, or a colleague from a partner organization who is accusing you of not holding up your end of an agreement, approach the issue in the same way.

Don't overcompensate

It's tempting to treat the situation differently than fighting with someone inside your organization. You might think, "This is a key supplier. I should do whatever it takes to smooth over this disagreement" or "They're just a vendor. We can find a new one next week." You may feel less invested in the relationship because there are 10 vendors who want your business. But although you may have lots of alternatives, know what it would mean to pursue them. Sometimes the cost of switching vendors or suppliers is higher than you think. "With external parties, you don't want to fall on your sword, but you also don't want to treat them as if they don't matter," says Jeff Weiss.

Show respect

With people you don't see regularly, and perhaps with whom you communicate mostly via email, it's important to demonstrate that you value the relationship. This isn't always implicit. It's a good way to signal that you're invested in working through the issue. Plus, it establishes a foundation of trust from which you can solve the problem: "I know we don't see each other often, but I wanted you to know that I value this relationship and appreciate what your company does for ours."

Jointly diagnose the problem

As with any conflict, you want to understand what the root cause is, but because you work in different organizations, you may know less about your counterpart, his perspective, and his goals. Sit down to jointly diagnose what led to the conflict. Is there a communication problem? Are you perceiving an issue differently? What about your contribution to the issues? Have you not given the supplier clear instructions? Have you been too hands-off? Have you made it difficult for him to do his job?

Know your counterpart's stakeholders

You likely have a contact at your supplier, but this isn't the person who makes all of the decisions that affect you. You're frustrated that he's not getting back to you about pricing or delivery terms, but it may be that he's trying to get his boss or finance on board with the new terms. "You are at the interface of the conflict," says Jonathan Hughes. When you do the work to better understand your counterpart and your goals, don't just focus on your point of contact. Also consider anyone who may have a stake in the decision. And when you propose a resolution, figure out how you can help your contact sell it internally at his organization so that it fits into their goals. You can ask, "How can I help you get approval for this arrangement?"

Consider the precedent

Because you may have fewer interactions with this person than you do with coworkers, it's important to examine the tone you're setting as it's likely to influence any discussions that come next. "Think about the history you want to have behind you," advises Weiss. If you mistreat your counterpart, you're sending the message that he can do the same the next time an issue comes up between your two organizations—whereas if you are thoughtful and respectful, and take his (and his company's) perspective into consideration, you're paving the way for smoother interactions in the future.

Zach's story

As the project manager at a building company, Zach works with dozens of subcontractors at a time—plumbers, painters, carpenters, electricians. "I approach these relationships with one question in mind: 'How can we partner to get this project done for a client?'" he says. But he acknowledges that it's difficult to settle disputes because the subcontractors can walk away from the job. "They don't have the relationship with the client; I do," he says.

A plumber with whom he was working on a big redesign project was getting upset about the payment terms. "It's standard in the industry to pay subcontractors within 30 days, but we're not always able to do that," Zach says. The plumber had put a lot of time and material into the project, and he hadn't received any payment. "The trouble was that the client wasn't paying us, so we couldn't pay out our subs." The plumber threatened to walk off the job.

Although Zach knew he could find another subcontractor if necessary, he valued his relationship with this plumber and said so. He told him, "Look, you've always been a great partner, and as you know, we typically pay net 30, but we're stuck in a bind this time. Can you see it from my perspective? I'd love to pay you, but I just don't have the money." Zach then offered to let him know as soon as the client check came in. "I promised I'd send him his check the very same day," he says. "I don't think he was happy with the outcome because he still had to wait for his money, but he understood the position I was in."

Knowing how to manage conflict at work won't make it go away, but it will make dealing with any disagreements easier and less stressful. Whether you're experiencing conflict with your direct report or your boss—or someone outside your business—you now have the tools to assess the situation and choose an approach that works for you. As these scenarios show, directly addressing the conflict is just one alternative. You also need to know when to walk away or get out of the relationship altogether. But if you do choose to sit down with your counterpart, you're now better equipped to prepare for and engage in a difficult conversation, manage your and your counterpart's emotions, and develop a resolution together.

Sources

Introduction

- Karen Dillon, *HBR Guide to Office Politics*, Harvard Business Review Press, 2015.

- Jennifer Lawler, "The Real Cost of Workplace Conflict," Entrepreneur.com, June 10, 2010, http://www.entrepreneur.com/article/207196.

- Kenneth W. Thomas, "Making Conflict Management a Strategic Advantage," CPP, https://www.cpp.com/pdfs/conflict_whitepaper.pdf.

- Jeanne Whalen, "Angry Outbursts Really Do Hurt Your Health, Doctors Find," *Wall Street Journal*, March 23, 2015, http://www.wsj.com/articles/angry-outbursts-really-do-hurt-your-health-doctors-find-1427150596.

Chapter 1

- Annie McKee, "How Power Affects Your Productivity," HBR.org, February 9, 2015, https://hbr.org/2015/02/how-power-affects-your-productivity.

Chapter 2

- Jeanne Brett, "When and How to Let a Conflict Go," HBR.org, June 10, 2014, https://hbr.org/2014/06/when-and-how-to-let-a-conflict-go/.

Chapter 3

- Hannah Riley Bowles, "Why Women Don't Negotiate Their Job Offers," HBR.org, June 19, 2014, https://hbr.org/2014/06/why-women-dont-negotiate-their-job-offers.

- Liane Davey, "Conflict Strategies for Nice People," HBR.org, December 25, 2013, https://hbr.org/2013/12/conflict-strategies-for-nice-people/.

- Judith E. Glaser, "Your Brain Is Hooked on Being Right," HBR.org, February 28, 2013, https://hbr.org/2013/02/break-your-addiction-to-being/.

- Amy Jen Su, "Get Over Your Fear of Conflict," HBR.org, June 6, 2014, https://hbr.org/2014/06/get-over-your-fear-of-conflict.

Chapter 4

- Jeanne Brett, "When and How to Let a Conflict Go," HBR.org, June 10, 2104, https://hbr.org/2014/06/when-and-how-to-let-a-conflict-go/.

- Ben Dattner, "Most Work Conflicts Aren't Due to Personality," HBR.org, May 20, 2014, https://hbr

.org/2014/05/most-work-conflicts-arent-due-to
-personality/.

- Karen Dillon, *HBR Guide to Office Politics,* Harvard Business Review Press, 2015.

- Jeffrey Pfeffer, "Win at Workplace Conflict," HBR.org, May 29, 2014, https://hbr.org/2014/05/win-at-workplace-conflict/.

- Judith White, "Two Kinds of People You Should Never Negotiate With," HBR.org, June 18, 2014, https://hbr.org/2014/06/two-kinds-of-people-you-should-never-negotiate-with/.

Chapter 5

- Jeanne Brett, "When and How to Let a Conflict Go," HBR.org, June 10, 2014, https://hbr.org/2014/06/when-and-how-to-let-a-conflict-go/.

- Susan David, "Manage a Difficult Conversation with Emotional Intelligence," HBR.org, June 19, 2014, https://hbr.org/2014/manage-a-difficult-conversation-with-emotional-intelligence/.

- Susan David and Christina Congleton, "Emotional Agility," *Harvard Business Review*, November 2013 (product R1311L).

- Amy Gallo, "Choose the Right Words in an Argument," HBR.org, June 16, 2014, https://hbr.org/2014/06/choose-the-right-words-in-an-argument/.

- Amy Gallo, "How to Work with Someone You Hate," HBR.org, January 30, 2012, https://hbr.org/2012/01/how-to-work-with-someone-you-h/.

- Amy Gallo, "The Right Way to Fight," HBR.org, May 12, 2010, https://hbr.org/2010/05/the-right-way-to-fight/.

- Rebecca Knight, "How to Handle Difficult Conversations at Work," HBR.org, January 9, 2015, https://hbr.org/2015/01/how-to-handle-difficult-conversations-at-work.

Chapter 6

- Dorie Clark, "How to Repair a Damaged Professional Relationship," HBR.org, June 5, 2014, https://hbr.org/2014/06/how-to-repair-a-damaged-professional-relationship.

- Liane Davey, "Conflict Strategies for Nice People," HBR.org, December 25, 2013, https://hbr.org/2013/12/conflict-strategies-for-nice-people/.

- Susan David and Christina Congleton, "Emotional Agility," *Harvard Business Review*, November 2013 (product R1311L).

- Amy Gallo, "Choose the Right Words in an Argument," HBR.org, June 16, 2014, https://hbr.org/2014/06/hoose-the-right-words-in-an-argument/.

- Amy Gallo, "The Right Way to Fight," HBR.org, May 12, 2010, https://hbr.org/2010/05/the-right-way-to-fight/.

- Mark Gerzon, "To Resolve a Conflict, First Decide: Is It Hot or Cold?" HBR.org, June 26, 2014, https://hbr.org/2014/06/to-resolve-a-conflict-first-decide-is-it-hot-or-cold/.

- Rebecca Knight, "How to Handle Difficult Conversations at Work," HBR.org, January 9, 2015, https://hbr.org/2015/01/how-to-handle-difficult-conversations-at-work.

- Katie Liljenquist and Adam Galinsky, "Win Over an Opponent by Asking for Advice," HBR.org, June 27, 2014, https://hbr.org/2014/06/win-over-an-opponent-by-asking-for-advice.

Chapter 7

- Rebecca Knight, "How to Handle Difficult Conversations at Work," HBR.org, January 9, 2015, https://hbr.org/2015/01/how-to-handle-difficult-conversations-at-work.

- Jeff Weiss, *HBR Guide to Negotiating,* Harvard Business Review Press, 2016.

Chapter 8

- Jeanne Brett, "When and How to Let a Conflict Go," HBR.org, June 10, 2014, https://hbr.org/2014/06/when-and-how-to-let-a-conflict-go/.

Sources

- Dorie Clark, "How to Repair a Damaged Professional Relationship," HBR.org, June 5, 2014, https://hbr.org/2014/06/how-to-repair-a-damaged-professional-relationship.

- Amy Gallo, "Fixing a Work Relationship Gone Sour," HBR.org, August 20, 2014, https://hbr.org/2014/08/fixing-a-work-relationship-gone-sour/.

- Amy Gallo, "How to Build the Social Ties You Need at Work," HBR.org, September 23, 2015, https://hbr.org/2015/09/how-to-build-the-social-ties-you-need-at-work.

- Amy Gallo, "How to Deal with a Mean Colleague," HBR.org, October 16, 2014, https://hbr.org/2014/10/how-to-deal-with-a-mean-colleague/.

- Amy Gallo, "How to Manage Someone You Don't Like," HBR.org, August 29, 2013, https://hbr.org/2013/08/how-to-manage-someone-you-dont/.

- Amy Gallo, "How to Work with Someone You Hate," HBR.org, January 30, 2012, https://hbr.org/2012/01/how-to-work-with-someone-you-h/.

- Caroline Webb, "How to Tell a Coworker They're Annoying You," HBR.org, March 10, 2016, https://hbr.org/2016/03/how-to-tell-a-coworker-theyre-annoying-you.

Chapter 9

- Jeanne Brett, "When and How to Let a Conflict Go," HBR.org, June 10, 2014, https://hbr.org/2014/06/when-and-how-to-let-a-conflict-go/.

- Liane Davey, "Conflict Strategies for Nice People," HBR.org, December 25, 2013, https://hbr.org/2013/12/conflict-strategies-for-nice-people/.

- Liane Davey, "Managing Two People Who Hate Each Other," HBR.org, June 9, 2014, https://hbr.org/2014/06/managing-two-people-who-hate-each-other/.

- Liane Davey, "What to Do When Your Boss Doesn't Like You," HBR.org, December 8, 2014, https://hbr.org/2014/12/what-to-do-when-your-boss-doesnt-like-you.

- Karen Dillon, "Don't Hide When Your Boss Is Mad at You," HBR.org, June 11, 2014, https://hbr.org/2014/06/dont-hide-when-your-boss-is-mad-at-you/.

- Nathanael J. Fast, Ethan R. Burris, and Caroline A. Bartel, "Research: Insecure Managers Don't Want Your Suggestions," HBR.org, November 24, 2014, https://hbr.org/2014/11/research-insecure-managers-dont-want-your-suggestions/.

- Keith Ferrazzi, "How to Manage Conflict in Virtual Teams," HBR.org, November 19, 2012, https://hbr.org/2012/11/how-to-manage-conflict-in-virt/.

- Amy Gallo, "Choose the Right Words in an Argument," HBR.org, June 16, 2014, https://hbr.org/2014/06/choose-the-right-words-in-an-argument/.

- Amy Gallo, "Get Your Team to Stop Fighting and Start Working," HBR.org, June 9, 2010, https://hbr.org/2010/06/get-your-team-to-stop-fighting/.

- Amy Gallo, "How to Deal with a Mean Colleague," HBR.org, October 16, 2014, https://hbr.org/2014/10/how-to-deal-with-a-mean-colleague.

- Amy Gallo, "The Right Way to Fight," HBR.org, May 12, 2010, https://hbr.org/2010/05/the-right-way-to-fight/.

- Amy Gallo, "When Two of Your Coworkers Are Fighting," HBR.org, July 3, 2014, https://hbr.org/2014/07/when-two-of-your-coworkers-are-fighting/.

- Amy Gallo, "When You Think the Strategy Is Wrong," HBR.org, February 4, 2010, https://hbr.org/2010/02/when-you-think-the-strategy-is.html.

- Daniel Goleman, "E-Mail Is Easy to Write (and to Misread)," *New York Times*, October 7, 2007, http://www.nytimes.com/2007/10/07/jobs/07pre.html?_r=0.

- Joseph Grenny, "How to Disagree with Your Boss," HBR.org, November 25, 2014, https://hbr.org/2014/11/how-to-disagree-with-your-boss.

- Joseph Grenny, "The Best Teams Hold Themselves Accountable," HBR.org, May 30, 2014, https://hbr.org/2014/05/the-best-teams-hold-themselves-accountable.

- Pamela Hinds, "4 Ways to Decrease Conflict Within Global Teams," HBR.org, June 27, 2014, https://hbr.org/2014/06/4-ways-to-decrease-conflict-within-global-teams.

- Amy Jen Su and Muriel Maignan Wilkins, "How to Deal with a Passive-Aggressive Peer," HBR.org, December 14, 2010, https://hbr.org/2010/12/how-to-deal-with-a-passive-agg.

- Rebecca Knight, "How to Manage Remote Direct Reports," HBR.org, February 10, 2015, https://hbr.org/2015/02/how-to-manage-remote-direct-reports.

- Annie McKee, "When Fighting with Your Boss, Protect Yourself First," HBR.org, July 22, 2014, https://hbr.org/2014/07/when-fighting-with-your-boss-protect-yourself-first/.

- Holly Weeks, "Say No Without Burning Bridges," HBR.org, June 24, 2014, https://hbr.org/2014/06/say-no-without-burning-bridges/.

Featured Experts

Deborah Ancona is the Seley Distinguished Professor of Management at the MIT Sloan School of Management and the faculty director of the MIT Leadership Center. She is also a coauthor of *X-Teams: How to Build Teams That Lead, Innovate, and Succeed* (with Henrik Bresman).

Richard Boyatzis is a Distinguished University Professor, and a professor in the departments of Organizational Behavior and Psychology Cognitive Science at Case Western Reserve University, where his MOOC "Inspiring Leadership Through Emotional Intelligence," has over 400,000 participants from over 200 countries. He is a coauthor of *Primal Leadership: Unleashing the Power of Emotional Intelligence* (with Daniel Goleman and Annie McKee), as well as *Resonant Leadership: Renewing Yourself and Connecting with Others Through Mindfulness, Hope, and Compassion* (with Annie Mckee) and *Becoming a Resonant Leader: Develop Your Emotional Intelligence, Renew Your Relationships, Sustain Your Effectiveness* (with Annie McKee and Fran Johnston).

Jeanne Brett is the DeWitt W. Buchanan, Jr. Distinguished Professor of Dispute Resolution and Organizations at the Kellogg School of Management, Northwestern University, and the director of the Kellogg School's Dispute Resolution Research Center. She is the author of *Negotiating Globally: How to Negotiate Deals, Resolve Disputes, and Make Decisions Across Cultural Boundaries* and a coauthor (with William Ury and Stephen B. Goldberg) of *Getting Disputes Resolved: Designing Systems to Cut the Costs of Conflict.*

Dorie Clark is a marketing strategist and professional speaker who teaches at Duke University's Fuqua School of Business. She is the author of *Reinventing You: Define Your Brand, Imagine Your Future* and *Stand Out: How to Find Your Breakthrough Idea and Build a Following Around It.* She is currently writing a book on being an entrepreneur for Harvard Business Review Press. You can access her free articles at dorieclark.com

Ben Dattner is an executive coach and the founder of Dattner Consulting in New York City. He is also the author of *The Blame Game: How the Hidden Rules of Credit and Blame Determine Our Success or Failure.*

Liane Davey is the cofounder of 3COze Inc. She is the author of *You First: Inspire Your Team to Grow Up, Get Along, and Get Stuff Done* and a coauthor (with David S. Weiss and Vince Molinaro) of *Leadership Solutions: The Pathway to Bridge the Leadership Gap.* Follow her on Twitter: @LianeDavey.

Susan David, PhD, a founder of the Harvard affiliated Institute of Coaching and CEO of Evidence Based Psychology, is an internationally recognized leader operating at the nexus of business and psychology. She routinely consults, speaks, and coaches at the most senior levels of *Fortune* 500 organizations and influential not-for-profits. She is the author of *Emotional Agility: Get Unstuck, Embrace Change, and Thrive in Work and Life* and coauthor of the definitive *Oxford Handbook of Happiness* (with Ilona Boniwell and Amanda Conley Ayers) and *Beyond Goals: Effective Strategies for Coaching and Mentoring* (with David Clutterbuck and David Megginson).

Karen Dillon is the author of the *HBR Guide to Office Politics* and a coauthor of *Competing Against Luck: The Story of Innovation and Customer Choice* (with Clayton M. Christensen, Taddy Hall, and David S. Duncan) and *How Will You Measure Your Life?* (with Clayton M. Christensen and James Allworth). She is the former editor of *Harvard Business Review*. Follow her on Twitter: @DillonHBR.

Nathanael Fast is an associate professor of management at the Marshall School of Business at the University of Southern California. He studies power and status in groups and organizations.

Keith Ferrazzi is the CEO of Ferrazzi Greenlight, a research-based consulting and coaching company, and the author of *Never Eat Alone* and the #1 best seller

Who's Got Your Back: The Breakthrough Program to Build Deep, Trusting Relationships That Create Success—and Won't Let You Fail.

Adam Galinsky is the Vikram S. Pandit Professor of Business and the chair of the Management Department at the Columbia Business School. He is the coauthor (with Maurice Schweitzer) of *Friend and Foe: When to Cooperate, When to Compete, and How to Succeed at Both*. His research focuses on leadership, power, negotiations, decision making, and ethics.

Mark Gerzon is the author of *Leading Through Conflict: How Successful Leaders Transform Differences into Opportunities* and the president of the Mediators Foundation.

Judith E. Glaser is the CEO of Benchmark Communications and the chairman of the Creating WE Institute. She is the author of six books, including *Creating WE: Change I-Thinking to We-Thinking and Build a Healthy, Thriving Organization* and *Conversational Intelligence: How Great Leaders Build Trust and Get Extraordinary Results*.

Daniel Goleman is a codirector of the Consortium for Research on Emotional Intelligence in Organizations at Rutgers University, a coauthor (with Richard Boyatzis and Annie McKee) of *Primal Leadership: Unleashing the Power of Emotional Intelligence,* and the author of *Focus: The Hidden Driver of Success, Emotional*

Intelligence: Why It Can Matter More Than IQ, The Brain and Emotional Intelligence: New Insights, and *Leadership: The Power of Emotional Intelligence, Selected Writings.*

Joseph Grenny is a cofounder of VitalSmarts, an innovator in corporate training and leadership development, and a coauthor of *Crucial Conversations: Tools for Talking When Stakes Are High* and *Crucial Accountability: Tools for Resolving Violated Expectations, Broken Commitments, and Bad Behavior* (with Kerry Patterson, Ron McMillan, and Al Switzler), as well as *Influencer: The New Science of Leading Change* and *Change Anything: The New Science of Personal Success* (with Kerry Patterson, David Maxfield, Ron McMillan, and Al Switzler).

Linda Hill is the Wallace Brett Donham Professor of Business Administration at Harvard Business School. She is a coauthor of *Being the Boss: The 3 Imperatives for Becoming a Great Leader* (with Kent Lineback) and *Collective Genius: The Art and Practice of Leading Innovation* (with Greg Brandeau, Emily Truelove, and Kent Lineback).

Pamela Hinds is a professor in management science and engineering at Stanford University. She studies the dynamics of globally distributed work teams and writes about issues of culture, language, and the transfer of work practices in global collaborations.

Jonathan Hughes is a partner at Vantage Partners, a global consultancy that advises companies on complex

B2B negotiations, strategic alliances, customer and supplier partnerships, and organizational transformation.

Amy Jen Su is a cofounder and managing partner of Paravis Partners, a boutique executive coaching and leadership development firm. She is a coauthor (with Muriel Maignan Wilkins) of *Own the Room: Discover Your Signature Voice to Master Your Leadership Presence*.

Roderick Kramer is the William R. Kimball Professor of Organizational Behavior, Stanford Graduate School of Business, a coeditor (with Todd Pittinsky) of *Restoring Trust in Organizations and Leaders*, and a coeditor (with George Goethals, Scott Allison, and David Messick) of *Conceptions of Leadership*.

Katie Liljenquist is on the faculty of Brigham Young University's Department of Organizational Leadership and Strategy. She studies decision making and interpersonal influence.

Muriel Maignan Wilkins is a cofounder and managing partner of Paravis Partners, a boutique executive coaching and leadership development firm. She is a coauthor (with Amy Jen Su) of *Own the Room: Discover Your Signature Voice to Master Your Leadership Presence*.

Jean-François Manzoni is the president and Nestlé Professor at IMD. He is a coauthor (with Jean-Louis Barsoux) of *The Set-Up-to-Fail Syndrome: How Good Managers Cause Great People to Fail*.

Annie McKee is a senior fellow at the University of Pennsylvania, the director of the PennCLO Executive Doctoral Program, and the founder of the Teleos Leadership Institute. She is a coauthor of *Primal Leadership: Unleashing the Power of Emotional Intelligence* (with Daniel Goleman and Richard Boyatzis), as well as *Resonant Leadership: Renewing Yourself and Connecting with Others Through Mindfulness, Hope, and Compassion* (with Richard Boyatzis), and *Becoming a Resonant Leader: Develop Your Emotional Intelligence, Renew Your Relationships, Sustain Your Effectiveness* (with Richard Boyatzis and Fran Johnston). She is also the author of the forthcoming *How to Be Happy at Work: The Power of Purpose, Hope, and Friendship.*

Erin Meyer is a professor specializing in cross-cultural management at INSEAD. She is the author of *The Culture Map: Breaking Through the Invisible Boundaries of Global Business.* Follow her @ErinMeyerINSEAD.

Mark Mortensen is an associate professor of organizational behavior at INSEAD. His work focuses on the changing nature of collaboration, particularly fluid, interdependent, and global teams.

Gary Namie is the founder of the Workplace Bullying Institute. He is a coauthor (with Ruth F. Namie) of *The Bully-Free Workplace: Stop Jerks, Weasels, and Snakes from Killing Your Organization* and *The Bully at Work: What You Can Do to Stop the Hurt and Reclaim Your Dignity on the Job.*

Jeffrey Pfeffer is Thomas D. Dee II Professor of Organizational Behavior at the Graduate School of Business,
Stanford University. He is the author of *Leadership BS:
Fixing Workplaces and Careers One Truth at a Time*,
and *Power: Why Some People Have It and Others Don't.*

Anna Ranieri is a career counselor, an executive coach,
and a coauthor (with Joe Gurkoff) of *How Can I Help?
What You Can (and Can't) Do to Counsel a Friend, Colleague, or Family Member with a Problem.*

Dr. John Ratey is an associate clinical professor of psychiatry at Harvard Medical School. He is the author of *A
User's Guide to the Brain.* He is also a coauthor of *Spark:
The Revolutionary New Science of Exercise and the Brain*
(with Eric Hagerman) and *Driven to Distraction: Recognizing and Coping with Attention Deficit Disorder from
Childhood Through Adulthood, Answers to Distraction,*
and *Delivered from Distraction: Getting the Most Out
of Life with Attention Deficit Disorder* (with Edward M.
Hallowell, MD).

Robert Sutton is a professor of management science and
engineering in the Stanford Engineering School, where
he is a cofounder and active member of the Stanford
Technology Ventures Program, and the Hasso Plattner
Institute of Design (the "d.school"). He is author or coauthor of six books, including *Good Boss, Bad Boss: How
to Be the Best . . . and Learn from the Worst* and *The No
Asshole Rule: Building a Civilized Workplace and Sur-*

viving One That Isn't, and *Scaling Up Excellence: Getting to More Without Settling for Less* (with Huggy Rao).

Brian Uzzi is the Richard L. Thomas Professor of Leadership and Organizational Change at Northwestern's Kellogg School of Management and the codirector of the Northwestern Institute on Complex Systems (NICO). He is a coauthor (with Shannon Dunlap) of the *Harvard Business Review* article "Make Your Enemies Your Allies."

Caroline Webb is the author of *How to Have a Good Day: Harness the Power of Behavioral Science to Transform Your Working Life.* She is also CEO of the coaching firm Sevenshift and a senior adviser to McKinsey & Company.

Holly Weeks is a communications consultant, an adjunct lecturer in public policy at the Harvard Kennedy School, and the author of *Failure to Communicate: How Conversations Go Wrong and What You Can Do to Right Them.*

Jeff Weiss is a partner at Vantage Partners, a global consultancy specializing in corporate negotiations, relationship management, partnering, and complex change management. He serves on the faculties of the Tuck School of Business at Dartmouth and the United States Military Academy at West Point, where he is also the codirector of the West Point Negotiation Project. He is author of the *HBR Guide to Negotiating.*

Judith White is a visiting associate professor of management at the Tuck School of Business at Dartmouth. Her research focuses on gender and diversity in groups, multidisciplinary teams, narcissism and negotiation, and conflict management.

Michele Woodward is a Master Certified Coach who coaches executives and trains other coaches.

Index

accountability, 90
active listening, 85–88
addressing conflict, options for,
    xxiv, xxv, 15–29, 52–58
advice
    asking for, 78–79, 88
    giving, 139
African cultures, conflict man-
    agement in, 20. *See also*
    cultural norms and
    conflict
anger
    health problems caused by,
    xx–xxi (*see also* health prob-
    lems related to conflict)
    toward boss, 141–145
    See also emotions
apologies, 90–92, 116–117
Asian cultures, indirect conflict
    handling in, 19–20, 36. *See*
    also cultural norms and
    conflict
assertive cultures, 23. *See*
    also cultural norms and
    conflict
assessment
    of counterpart, 43–47

of situation, 43–60
avoidance of conflict, xx, 17, 21
avoiders, conflict, xxv, 32–34, 48

back pain, 33. *See also* health
    problems related to conflict
benefits of conflict, xxi–xxiii
blame
    admitting, 90
    assigning, 76
body
    focusing on your, 82
    language, 91–93, 94
boss
    anger toward, 141–145
    colleague goes over your head
    to, 130–136
    escalating conflict to, 108
    repairing relationship with, 134
    respect for, 142–143
brainstorming, resolution, 105.
    See also conflict resolution
breaks
    from difficult conversations,
    83, 108
    from work, 112

breathing, deep, 82. *See also* calmness

bullies, dealing with, 145–148

calmness, 81–83, 95. *See also* emotions

causes of conflict, roots of, xxiii–xxiv, 3, 12–13

collaboration, and resolutions, 105. *See also* conflict resolution

colleagues
    bullying by, 145–148
    caught in middle of warring, 136–141
    going over your head by, 130–136
    who hate each other, 152–157
    See also counterpart

commonalities, focusing on, 117. *See also* conflict resolution

common ground
    focusing on, 76–77 (*see also* conversations)
    identifying, 49–50 (*see also* assessment of situation)

common situations, navigating. *See* conflict situations

communication
    clarifying lines of, 133–134
    during conversations, 89–95, 96
    email, 122–126
    informal, 124–125
    nonverbal, 92–93, 94

conflict avoiders, xxv, 32–34, 48

conflict management
    adapting approach to, 59–60
    direct option for, xxiv, 22–25, 53

do-nothing option for, xxiv, 15–19, 53
    exit option for, xxiv, 25–28, 53, 57–58
    indirect option for, xxiv, 19–22, 53
    involving third parties in, 20, 95–97
    lead by counterpart, 28–29
    plan for, xxiii–xxviii
    situation assessment, 43–60
    win-win approach to, xxiii

conflict resolution, 101–110
    accepting lack of, 107–109
    characteristics of, 101–103
    documenting agreement, 107
    evaluating possibilities, 105–106
    fairness and reasonableness of, 103
    reaching, 103–107
    satisfying interests in, 102–103

conflict seekers, xxv, 32, 34–35, 48

conflict situations, 121–164
    anger toward boss, 141–145
    caught in middle of warring colleagues, 136–141
    colleague goes over your head, 130–136
    counterpart with mental illness, 148–152
    dealing with bullies, 145–148
    fighting from afar, 122–126
    managing people who hate each other, 152–157
    passive-aggressive counterparts, 126–130
    with someone outside of office, 160–164
    team turns on you, 157–160

conflict types, xxiv, xxv, 3–13, 47,
    49–50, 77–78
context and conflict, organiza-
    tional, 64–65
contrary opinions, express-
    ing, 91–92. *See also*
    communication
conversations
    asking questions during,
        86–88
    being heard during, 89–95
    changing tenor of, 93, 95
    choosing place for, 68–69, 72
    delaying, 28–29, 57, 68, 72
    email, 122–126
    framing, xxvii, 75, 76–80
    lack of time to prepare for,
        70, 72
    listening during, 85–88
    managing emotions during,
        80–85
    mindset for, 61–62, 71
    multiple scenarios for, 66, 71
    planning message for, 65–66,
        71
    pre-conversation checklist,
        71–72
    preparing for, xxvi, 61–73
    productive, xxvii, 75–98
    setting ground rules for, 79
    structuring, 50
    taking break from, 83
    timing of, 66–68, 72
    venting before, 69–70, 71
counterpart
    body language of, 92–93, 94
    common ground with, 49–50,
        76–77
    conversations with (*see*
        conversations)
    empathy for, 117–118

input from others on, 45
listening to, 85–88
with mental illness, 148–152
passive-aggressive, 126–130
perspective of, 88
providing feedback to, 118–119
repairing relationship with,
    111–120
stakeholders of, 162
taking perspective of, 62–63,
    71
understanding your, 43–47, 124
venting by, 83–85
coworkers. *See* colleagues;
    counterpart
creativity, to reach resolu-
    tion, 104. *See also* conflict
    resolution
cultural bridges, 45
cultural differences, 122–123
cultural norms and conflict,
    19–20, 36, 45, 46, 64,
    75–76

deadlines, 67. *See also* timing, of
    conversations
decision making and resolu-
    tions, 106. *See also* conflict
    resolution
deep breathing, 82. *See also*
    calmness
defensiveness, 76. *See also* con-
    versations, productive
diabetes, xxi. *See also* health
    problems related to conflict
difficult conversations. *See*
    conversations
direct confrontation, xxiv, 22–25,
    53. *See also* options for
    addressing conflict

disagreements, unspoken, xx. *See also* conflict avoiders

discussions. *See* conversations

doing nothing, as option for addressing conflict, xxiv, 15–19, 53. *See also* options for addressing conflict

downsides of conflict, xix–xxi

email, 69, 122–126. *See also* communication; location, for conversations

emotional leakage, 70. *See also* emotions

emotional reactions, 49, 54, 55, 58

emotional toll, of conflict, xx–xxi. *See also* health problems related to conflict

emotions
  acknowledging, 83
  checking, before conversations, 67–68
  during conflict resolution, 106
  labeling, 83
  management of, 80–85
  negative, xxvii
  suppressing, 70
  venting, 83–85

empathy, 117–118, 138. *See also* relationships, repairing

escalating conflict, to boss, 108

exiting, as option for addressing conflict, 25–28, 53, 57–58. *See also* options for addressing conflict

experiences with conflict, past, 36

external partners, conflicts with, 160–164

face saving, 19, 21. *See also* options for addressing conflict

feedback
  asking for, on conflict style, 39
  providing, 118–119

fighting-from-afar situation, 122–126

fight-or-flight response, 54, 81. *See also* emotions

finger-pointing, 90. *See also* conversations, productive

future, focusing on, 79–80, 112–113

gender norms, 37. *See also* natural tendencies, for handling conflict

goals
  determining your, 51–52
  disputes over, 4, 7–9
  returning to original, 95
  shared, 65, 76–77, 128

ground rules for difficult conversations, 79. *See also* conversations, productive

growth opportunities, xxii. *See also* benefits of conflict

headaches, 33. *See also* health problems related to conflict

health problems related to conflict, xx–xxi, 33. *See also* emotional toll, of conflict

heart attacks, xx. *See also* health problems related to conflict

hypotheticals, 92. *See also* conversations, productive

indirect confrontation, xxiv, 19–22, 53. *See also* options for addressing conflict

informal communication, 124–125. *See also* communication

innovation, xxi. *See also* benefits of conflict

interpersonal conflicts. *See* relationship conflicts

job satisfaction, xxii–xxiii. *See also* benefits of conflict

language
body, 92–93, 94
verbal, 90–92, 96

Latin American cultures, 36. *See also* cultural norms and conflict

learning opportunity, conflict as, xxii, 109–110. *See also* benefits of conflict

listening, active, 85–88

location, for conversations, 68–69, 72

mantras, 82. *See also* calmness

mediators, 97. *See also* conversations, productive

men, conflict styles and, 37

mental illness, and conflict, 148–152

messages
nonverbal, 92–93
planning, 65–66, 71

metaphors, 19–20. *See also* indirect confrontation

mindset, 61–62, 71

multiple scenarios, preparing for, 66, 71

Myers-Briggs Type Indicator (MBTI), 39. *See also* natural tendencies, for handling conflict

name-calling, 90. *See also* conversations, productive

National Alliance on Mental Illness, 150. *See also* mental illness, and conflict

natural tendencies, for handling conflict, xxiv–xxv, 31–40, 47, 48
assessing your counterpart's, 43–47
being mindful of, 54
conflict avoiders, xxv, 32–34, 48
conflict seekers, xxv, 34–35, 48
identifying your, 35–40
interactions between different styles, 47, 48
timing of conversations and, 67

negative emotions, xxvii, 80–85. *See also* emotions

nonverbal communication, 92–93, 94. *See also* communication

office context, 37, 45, 64–65

open mind, 62. *See also* mindset

options for addressing conflict, xxiv, xxv, 15–29, 52–58

organizational context, 64–65

organizational culture, 23, 64

outcomes, better work. *See* benefits of conflict

outside partners, conflicts with, 160–164

passive-aggressive counterparts, 126–130
personal disagreements, xxiv, xxv, 4, 5–7, 50. *See also* relationship conflicts
personality assessment, 39–40. *See also* natural tendencies, for handling conflict
perspective
    owning your, 89–90
    of your counterpart, 62–63, 71, 88
physical reactions, to conflict, 54, 81
power struggles, 95. *See also* conversations, productive
pre-conversation checklist, 71–72
process conflicts, xxiv, xxv, 4, 9–11, 101–102. *See also* conflict types
psychometric tests, 39–40. *See also* natural tendencies, for handling conflict

questions
    asking thoughtful, 86–88 (*see also* conversations, productive)
    rebuilding relationships through, 113, 116 (*see also* relationships, repairing)

rapport building, 113. *See also* relationships, repairing

rational thinking, 49, 54, 80–81
reciprocity, 116. *See also* relationships, repairing
relationship conflicts, xxiv, xxv, 4, 5–7, 50, 52, 89–90, 102, 106–107. *See also* conflict types
relationships
    with boss, 134, 141–145
    with colleagues, 130–141, 145–148
    exiting, xxiv, 25–28, 57–58
    improvements in, xxii (*see also* benefits of conflict)
    repairing, xxvii, 111–120, 134
remote, fighting with someone from afar, 122–126
resolution. *See* conflict resolution
role-playing, 47. *See also* counterpart, understanding your
root causes of conflict, xxiii–xxiv, 3, 12–13

scenarios, common. *See* conflict situations
seekers, conflict, xxv, 32, 34–35, 48
self-awareness, 38–39. *See also* natural tendencies, for handling conflict
situation assessment, 43–60
    goal setting, 51–52
    identifying type of conflict, 47, 49–50
    picking option for handling conflict, 52–58
    understanding your counterpart, 43–47
situations, common. *See* conflict situations

status conflicts, xxiv, xxv, 4, 11–12, 102. *See also* conflict types

stories, 19–20. *See also* indirect confrontation

stroke, xx. *See also* health problems related to conflict

suppliers, conflicts with, 160–164

sympathetic nervous system, 81. *See also* emotions

task conflicts, xxiv, xxv, 4, 7–9, 101. *See also* conflict types

team members
    who hate each other, 152–157
    who turn on you, 157–160

tendency for handling conflict, natural, xxiv–xxv, 31–40, 47, 48

third parties
    involving in conflict, 20, 95–97, 128–129, 159
    rebuilding relationships and, 118

Thomas-Kilmann Conflict Mode Instrument (TKI), 39–40. *See also* natural tendencies, for handling conflict

timing, of conversations, 66–68. *See also* conversations, productive

trust, restoring, 116. *See also* relationships, repairing

types of, conflict, xxiv, xxv, 3–13, 47, 49–50, 77–78

vendors, conflicts with, 160–164

venting, 69–70, 71, 83–85, 138

venue, for conversations, 68–69, 72

virtual teams, 122–126

walking away, from conflict, 55–58. *See also* options for addressing conflict

weight gain, 33. *See also* health problems related to conflict

women, conflict styles and, 37

work, conflict at, xvii–xix, xx, xxiii

work outcomes, better, xxi. *See also* benefits of conflict

workplace norms, 37, 45

About the Author

Amy Gallo is a contributing editor at *Harvard Business Review*, where she covers a range of topics including managing yourself, leading people, and building your career. As a speaker and workshop facilitator, Amy has helped dozens of organizations deal with conflict more effectively and navigate complicated workplace dynamics. Previously, she was a management consultant at Katzenbach Partners, a strategy and organization consulting firm. She is a graduate of Yale University and has a master's in public policy from Brown University. Follow her on Twitter @amyegallo.

Smart advice and inspiration from a source you trust.

If you enjoyed this book and want more comprehensive guidance on essential professional skills, turn to the HBR Guides Boxed Set. Packed with the practical advice you need to succeed, this seven-volume collection provides smart answers to your most pressing work challenges.

Harvard Business Review Guides

Available in paperback or ebook format. Plus, find downloadable tools and templates to help you get started.

- Better Business Writing
- Building Your Business Case
- Buying a Small Business
- Coaching Employees
- Delivering Effective Feedback
- Finance Basics for Managers
- Getting the Mentoring You Need
- Getting the Right Work Done

- Leading Teams
- Making Every Meeting Matter
- Managing Stress at Work
- Managing Up and Across
- Negotiating
- Office Politics
- Persuasive Presentations
- Project Management

HBR.ORG/GUIDES

Buy for your team, clients, or event.
Visit hbr.org/bulksales for quantity discount rates.

The most important management ideas all in one place.

We hope you enjoyed this book from *Harvard Business Review*. For the best ideas HBR has to offer turn to HBR's 10 Must Reads Boxed Set. From books on leadership and strategy to managing yourself and others, this 6-book collection delivers articles on the most essential business topics to help you succeed.

HBR's 10 Must Reads Series

The definitive collection of ideas and best practices on our most sought-after topics from the best minds in business.

- Change Management
- Collaboration
- Communication
- Emotional Intelligence
- Innovation
- Leadership
- Making Smart Decisions

- Managing Across Cultures
- Managing People
- Managing Yourself
- Strategic Marketing
- Strategy
- Teams
- The Essentials

hbr.org/mustreads

Buy for your team, clients, or event.
Visit hbr.org/bulksales for quantity discount rates.